GENDER INCLUSIVITY STANDARDS AND EXPECTATIONS IN HIGHER EDUCATION

A COMPREHENSIVE ASSESSMENT TOOL FOR GROWTH

JULIA G. MAKINSTER

LUCA E. LEWIS

JULIA MAKINSTER AND LUCA LEWIS PUBLISHING

Gender Inclusivity Standards and Expectations for Higher Education: A Comprehensive Assessment Tool for Growth and Advancement

Copyright © 2025 by Julia G. MaKinster and Luca E. Lewis

All rights reserved. No part of this publication may be reproduced, distributed, or transmitted in any form or by any means, including photocopying, recording, or other electronic or mechanical methods, without the prior written permission of the authors, except as permitted by U.S. copyright law and fair use standards.

Fair use of this work is permitted and encouraged for educational purposes, including but not limited to: classroom instruction, faculty and staff training, professional development workshops, conference presentations, and institutional policy development. Users may reproduce individual standards, assessment tools, or brief excerpts for these educational purposes, provided that proper attribution is given to the authors and this publication. For permissions beyond fair use, including reproduction of substantial portions for commercial purposes or wide distribution, please contact the authors.

Published by:

Julia G. MaKinster and Luca E. Lewis

Printed by IngramSpark in the United States of America

Formatted with Vellum

Cover Design by Asher Reed at Epic Story Publishing, Winter Park, FL

ISBN: 979-8-9931093-0-5 (paperback)

Library of Congress Control Number: 2025919561

First Edition: September, 2025

The authors and publisher have made every effort to ensure the accuracy of the information contained in this book. However, the information is provided "as is" without warranty of any kind, express or implied. The authors and publisher disclaim any liability for any damages resulting from the use of this information.

For permissions requests, bulk orders, or other inquiries, please contact: transcendconsultinggroupllc@gmail.com

Publisher's Cataloging-in-Publication

Provided by Cassidy Cataloguing Services, Inc.

Names: MaKinster, Julia G., author. | Lewis, Luca E., author.

Title: Gender inclusivity standards and expectations for higher education : a comprehensive assessment tool for growth and advancement / Julia G. MaKinster, Luca E. Lewis.

Description: [Farmington, New York] : Julia MaKinster and Luca Lewis Publishing, [2025] | Includes bibliographical references and index.

Identifiers: LCCN: 2025919561 | ISBN: 9798993109305 (paperback) | 9798993109312 (e-pub)

Subjects: LCSH: Educational equalization--Study and teaching (Higher)--Standards--United States. | Inclusive education--Study and teaching (Higher)--Standards--United States. | Education, Higher--Standards--United States. | Gender mainstreaming--Study and teaching (Higher)--Standards--United States. | Gender-blindness--Study and teaching (Higher)--Standards--United States. | Gender binary--Study and teaching (Higher)--Standards--United States. | Gender-nonconforming people--Education (Higher)--Standards--United States. | Transgender people--Education (Higher)--Standards--United States. | Transsexuals--Education (Higher)--Standards--United States. | BISAC: EDUCATION / Administration / Higher. | SOCIAL SCIENCE / Gender Studies. | EDUCATION / Administration / General.

Classification: LCC: LC213.2 .M35 2025 | DDC: 379.26/0973--dc23

CONTENTS

Notes	1
Chapter 1 *Introduction*	3
Chapter 2 *Theoretical Framework*	9
Standard 3 *Admissions Practices and Culture*	17
Standard 4 *Curriculum and Pedagogy*	27
Standard 5 *Student Life and Co-Curricular Engagement*	31
Standard 6 *Intersectionality*	37
Standard 7 *Recruiting and Retaining Gender-Expansive Employees*	43
Standard 8 *Institutional Policies and Practices*	49
Standard 9 *Campus Spaces*	55
Standard 10 *Administrative and Academic Offices, Centers, and Departments*	61
Standard 11 *Health and Wellness Services*	71
Standard 12 *Data Collection and Assessment*	77
Standard 13 *Executive Search Firms*	83
Chapter 14 *Toward a Future of Belonging and Excellence*	89
References	93
About the Authors	95
Index	97

NOTES

THE STANDARDS in this manuscript begin with standard number "three," so as to align with a forthcoming book, *Gender Inclusiveness and Belonging in Higher Education*. The book will include a chapter that focuses on the same topic as each of the eleven standards. We've chosen to start the standards numbering here so the standard numbers align with the book chapter numbers.

Please note that the Standards in this book are intentionally formatted as lists. Standards 3 through 13 are not necessarily meant to be read in order. They should be used as a guide for institutional assessment, professional development, and for short and long-term planning. We hope you find them to be useful.

CHAPTER 1
INTRODUCTION

IN THIS PIVOTAL moment in higher education, institutions across the nation face an unprecedented opportunity—and responsibility—to create cultures and environments where all members of their communities can thrive authentically. The standards and expectations presented in this document emerge from both an urgent need and a profound possibility: the demonstrated need to address systemic barriers that have historically marginalized transgender and gender-expansive individuals, and the opportunity to transform higher education into a space that truly embodies its commitments to learning, discovery, and human flourishing.

Higher education leaders have a moral imperative to respond to this moment in ways that are thoughtful and active. Ideally, they respond in ways that respect, if not celebrate, the dignity and humanity of gender-expansive people. Our hope is that these standards resonate with staff, faculty, and administrators of all types and at all levels of higher education institutions. No matter their position, the following standards will provide employees with approaches and practices that identify and challenge traditional gender norms and binaries in the hope of advancing greater inclusivity of gender identities and expressions. At the same time, the focus cannot be on pursuing specific goals or strategies alone. Rather, creating a gender-inclusive campus begins with a gender-inclusive mindset and an overall culture that informs interactions and decision-making with individuals, the design and execution of systems, and the leadership required within institutions of higher education to drive lasting, transformative change.

The comprehensive standards outlined in this document represent more than a collection of best practices—they constitute a roadmap for institutional transformation that recognizes gender diversity and inclusivity as fundamental to the educational mission. From the first moment a prospective student encounters an institution through admissions processes, to the daily experiences of learning, living, and working on campus, to the ongoing relationships maintained with alums and the broader community, these standards provide a framework for embedding gender inclusivity into every aspect of institutional life.

The Current Landscape and Urgent Need

These standards emerge from both research and lived experience that illuminate the significant challenges faced by transgender and gender-expansive individuals in higher education settings. National studies consistently demonstrate that students, faculty, and staff who identify outside traditional gender binaries encounter higher rates of low academic and work performance, discrimination, harassment, and exclusion within academic environments (James, et al., 2016; Kosciw, et al., 2022; Goldberg, et al., 2019). These experiences not only compromise individual well-being and success but also diminish the intellectual and social richness of our campus communities.

The consequences of gender-exclusive practices extend far beyond individual harm. When institutions fail to create inclusive environments, they lose the diverse perspectives, innovative thinking, and authentic contributions that gender-expansive community members bring to campus life, teaching, and scholarship. Moreover, the exclusion of any community member based on gender identity fundamentally contradicts higher education's stated commitments to equity, excellence, and the pursuit of knowledge.

Yet this moment also presents a remarkable opportunity. Across the country, institutions are recognizing that gender inclusivity is not merely a compliance issue or diversity initiative, but rather an essential component of educational excellence. When transgender and gender-expansive students feel safe, supported, and valued, they contribute more fully to classroom discussions, research endeavors, and campus communities. When faculty and staff can bring their authentic selves to their work, they model authenticity and resilience for students while advancing innovation and effectiveness. When institutional policies and practices affirm diverse gender identities, they create conditions for all community members to thrive.

The question of whether institutions should prioritize gender inclusivity when transgender and gender-expansive individuals represent approximately 1.7% of the U.S. population fundamentally misunderstands both the nature of institutional responsibility and the broader impact of inclusive practices. Just as universities would never consider abandoning accessibility accommodations because students with disabilities represent a numerical minority, the moral imperative for gender inclusion rests not on population statistics but on the fundamental principle of human dignity and the institutional commitment to creating environments where all community members can thrive. Furthermore, the impact of gender-inclusive practices extends far beyond those who identify as transgender or gender-expansive. When institutions embed inclusive practices into their systems and culture, they strengthen critical thinking skills across the campus community by challenging binary assumptions, foster innovation through diverse perspectives, and model the kind of thoughtful, respectful engagement with difference that is essential for democratic citizenship and global leadership. The exclusion of any community member based on identity dimensions diminishes the intellectual vitality and moral integrity of the entire institution, while inclusive practices create conditions that enhance learning, discovery, and authentic human connection for everyone.

The landscape of higher education evaluation is evolving to include considerations of gender inclusivity, though the direct institutional impacts remain largely unmeasured. Some ranking systems now incorporate gender equality metrics—such as QS Stars' assessment of gender diversity among students and faculty (Top Universities, 2024), and Times Higher Education's rankings based on UN Sustainable Development Goal 5 for gender equality (Times Higher Education, 2025). Student preferences also suggest growing expectations for institutional commitment to diversity, with surveys indicating that over half of students would consider transferring if their institution abolished DEI initiatives (Best Colleges, 2025). While these trends suggest that gender inclusivity may increasingly factor into institutional reputation and compliance requirements, research documenting direct causal relationships between inclusive policies and measurable outcomes like funding acquisition, faculty recruitment success, or operational cost savings remains limited. The question for institutional leaders is not whether they can afford to implement these practices, but whether they can navigate an evolving landscape where inclusivity is becoming a component of institutional student expectations and evaluation.

A Comprehensive Framework for Institutional Transformation

The standards presented are intentionally comprehensive, addressing eleven distinct yet interconnected domains of institutional practice. This breadth reflects a fundamental understanding: gender inclusivity cannot be achieved through isolated interventions or superficial policy changes. Instead, it requires systematic attention to how gender assumptions and binary thinking permeate every aspect of institutional culture and operations.

Beginning with admissions practices and extending through curriculum design, student life programming, employee recruitment and retention, health services, physical spaces, data collection, and executive leadership, these standards recognize that meaningful change must be both deep and wide. They acknowledge that prospective students' first encounters with institutional websites and application processes set expectations for the campus climate they will encounter. They understand that classroom experiences, residential life, and co-curricular engagement opportunities either affirm or alienate students based on how well they accommodate diverse gender identities. They recognize that the daily experiences of students, faculty, and staff—from restroom access to benefits policies to performance evaluation criteria—communicate institutional values about whose presence is welcome and valued.

Importantly, these standards also emphasize intersectionality, acknowledging that gender identity intersects with race, ethnicity, socioeconomic status, disability, nationality, and other aspects of identity in ways that shape individual experiences and institutional barriers. This intersectional framework ensures that efforts to advance gender inclusivity do not inadvertently perpetuate other forms of exclusion, instead working toward justice and belonging for all community members.

Implementation as an Ongoing Journey

The standards presented in this document are designed to be adaptable across diverse higher education institutional contexts—from large research universities to small liberal arts colleges, from community colleges to professional schools, from public institutions to private organizations. While the specific implementation strategies may vary based on institutional size, mission, resources, and community, the underlying commitment to gender inclusivity and the framework for comprehensive change remain consistent.

Successful implementation requires building institutional awareness, strategic planning, and cultural development. Institutions must assess their current practices, identify priority areas for improvement, allocate necessary resources, and establish accountability mechanisms. Equally important, they must cultivate campus-wide understanding of why this work matters, build capacity for inclusive practices, and create ongoing opportunities for community input and feedback.

The standards also recognize that implementation will be an iterative process. As understanding of gender diversity continues to evolve, as new challenges and opportunities emerge, and as institutional communities grow and change, these standards must be revisited, refined, and re-evaluated. At their core, these standards call for a fundamental shift in institutional culture—from one that assumes gender binary thinking to one that celebrates gender diversity, from reactive accommodation to proactive affirmation, from isolated diversity initiatives to integrated institutional transformation.

CHAPTER 2
THEORETICAL FRAMEWORK

THIS THEORETICAL FRAMEWORK emerges from decades of scholarship in gender studies, organizational change theory, critical pedagogy, and higher education administration, while centering the lived experiences and wisdom of transgender and gender-expansive communities (e.g., Butler, 1990; Freire, 1970/2000; Marine, 2011). The constructs explored in this chapter provide the conceptual foundation necessary to understand why superficial policy changes are insufficient and why meaningful transformation requires sustained attention to culture, systems, and individual mindset shifts.

The gender-inclusive standards presented in this volume rest upon a sophisticated theoretical foundation that challenges conventional approaches to diversity and inclusion in higher education. Rather than offering a simple checklist of policies to implement or boxes to check, these standards represent an integrated framework designed to facilitate deep, systemic cultural change over time. Utilizing the theoretical constructs that underpin this framework is essential for institutional leaders who seek not merely to comply with evolving expectations but to fundamentally transform their campus environments into spaces where all community members can authentically thrive.

Gender Identity and Gender Expression: Foundational Distinctions

Central to any gender-inclusive framework is a nuanced understanding of gender identity and gender expression as distinct yet related concepts.

Gender identity refers to an individual's internal, deeply held sense of their own gender—whether that aligns with the sex assigned at birth, differs from it, or exists outside traditional binary categories altogether (American Psychological Association, 2015). This internal sense of self is fundamental to human identity and cannot be determined by external observation or assumption. According to the American Psychological Association (2015), gender identity is "one's internal sense of being male, female, or something else."

Gender expression, by contrast, encompasses the external manifestation of gender through clothing, behavior, voice, body language, and other characteristics that may be culturally associated with particular genders (American Psychological Association, 2015). Gender expression is defined as "the outward manner in which an individual expresses or displays their gender" and may include "choices in clothing and hairstyle, or speech and mannerisms" (University of California San Francisco, 2016). Importantly, gender expression may or may not align with gender identity, and individuals may express their gender differently across contexts, relationships, and time periods.

The distinction between identity and expression is crucial for understanding why gender-inclusive practices must address both internal recognition and external accommodation. When institutions honor chosen names and pronouns, they acknowledge gender identity. When they eliminate binary dress codes or create flexible housing arrangements, they support diverse forms of gender expression. Effective gender inclusion requires attention to both dimensions.

Furthermore, these standards recognize that both gender identity and expression exist along continuums rather than within rigid categories. While some individuals identify clearly within traditional binary categories, others experience their gender as fluid, non-binary, or otherwise outside conventional frameworks (Goldberg & Kuvalanka, 2018). Gender-inclusive institutions must design systems and cultures that accommodate this full spectrum of human experience.

Intersectionality: The Complexity of Multiple Identity Dimensions

Intersectionality, a concept originated by legal scholar Kimberlé Crenshaw (1989), provides a critical lens for understanding how gender identity intersects with race, ethnicity, socioeconomic status, disability, nationality, sexual orientation, age, and other aspects of human identity. This theoretical framework recognizes that individuals do not experience gender identity in isolation, but rather as one dimension of a complex, multifaceted identity that shapes their interactions with institutional systems and cultural environments.

Crenshaw (1989) developed intersectionality to address "the marginalization of Black women within not only antidiscrimination law but also in feminist and antiracist theory and politics" (p. 139). She further elaborated that intersectionality reveals how multiple systems of oppression create experiences that are "greater than the sum of racism and sexism" (Crenshaw, 1991, p. 1244).

For gender-expansive individuals, intersectionality reveals how multiple systems of oppression may compound to create unique challenges and barriers. A transgender student of color may face both racism and transphobia, experiencing discrimination that differs qualitatively from what either a white transgender student or a cisgender student of color might encounter. Similarly, an international transgender student may navigate not only gender identity issues but also visa requirements, cultural differences, and potential conflicts with family or home country expectations.

Gender-inclusive institutions rely on policies, programs, and practices that recognize and respond to these intersecting identities. This means moving beyond one-size-fits-all approaches to create flexible, responsive systems that can accommodate the full complexity of human experience. It requires disaggregating data to understand differential impacts, creating affinity spaces for specific intersectional communities, and ensuring that efforts to advance gender inclusion do not inadvertently perpetuate other forms of marginalization.

Transformative Change

The theoretical framework underlying these standards recognizes that meaningful gender inclusion requires **transformative change** rather than superficial modifications (Marine, 2011). Such change requires attention to both **systemic and cultural change,** rather than relying solely on individual actions or isolated policy modifications. While individual awareness and competency are essential, lasting transformation occurs when entire institutional systems—policies, procedures, physical environments, communication practices, and organizational cultures—are redesigned and advanced to integrate gender inclusivity as a core value.

Systemic change involves examining and modifying the formal structures, policies, and procedures that govern institutional operations. This includes everything from admissions processes and academic records systems to housing policies and employee benefits. Systemic change recognizes that these formal structures often embed assumptions about gender that create barriers for gender-expansive individuals, even when discrimination is not intended.

Cultural change addresses the informal norms, shared assumptions, and everyday practices that shape campus climate and interpersonal interactions. Culture encompasses how people communicate with one another, what behaviors are celebrated or discouraged, how conflicts are resolved, and what messages are conveyed through both explicit and implicit means. Cultural change is often more challenging than systemic change because it requires shifts in mindset, behavior, and interpersonal dynamics across entire campus communities.

The interplay between systemic and cultural change is crucial. Policy changes without cultural transformation often result in superficial compliance without meaningful inclusion. Cultural shifts without systemic support may create positive interpersonal experiences while leaving structural barriers intact. Effective gender inclusion requires coordinated attention to both dimensions, recognizing that they reinforce and enable one another over time.

Gender-Inclusive Mindset

Moving beyond basic awareness or tolerance, the standards emphasize the development of a **gender-inclusive mindset** among all community members (Case et al., 2012). A gender-inclusive mindset represents a fundamental orientation toward viewing gender diversity as natural, valuable, and deserving of celebration rather than something to be managed or accommodated. This mindset involves several key components:

- Epistemic humility: Recognizing that one's own understanding of gender is limited and culturally situated, and maintaining openness to learning from others' experiences
- Critical consciousness: Developing awareness of how gender assumptions and binary thinking permeate institutional systems and personal interactions
- Proactive inclusion: Moving beyond reactive responses to discrimination toward proactive creation of inclusive environments

- Intersectional awareness: Understanding how gender intersects with other identity dimensions to shape individual experiences
- Growth orientation: Embracing continuous learning and adaptation rather than seeking fixed solutions or final answers

Developing a gender-inclusive mindset requires ongoing education, reflection, and practice. It cannot be achieved through single training sessions or policy orientations, but must be cultivated through sustained engagement with gender-expansive communities, regular self-reflection, and commitment to personal and professional growth.

Continuous Improvement and Adaptive Framework

Rather than viewing gender inclusion as a destination to be reached, **continuous improvement** and **adaptive capacity** are essential characteristics of inclusive institutions (Marine, 2011). This perspective recognizes that understanding of gender diversity continues to evolve, that individual and community needs change over time, and that institutional contexts shift in ways that require ongoing attention and refinement.

An adaptive framework approach involves several key elements:

- Regular assessment: Systematically evaluating the effectiveness of current policies and practices through data collection, community feedback, and outcome measurement
- Responsive modification: Adjusting approaches based on assessment findings, emerging research, and changing community needs
- Learning orientation: Treating challenges and mistakes as opportunities for growth rather than failures to be avoided
- Innovation capacity: Developing institutional capability to experiment with new approaches and adapt successful innovations from other contexts
- Future orientation: Anticipating emerging needs and trends rather than only responding to current challenges

This adaptive approach recognizes that the specific practices that constitute gender inclusion may change over time as understanding deepens and communities evolve. What remains constant is the commitment to creating environments where all individuals can thrive authentically and contribute fully to institutional mission.

Dignity and Belonging: Core Values and Outcomes

Underlying all aspects of the theoretical framework are the fundamental values of **human dignity** and **belonging.** These concepts provide both the moral foundation for gender inclusion efforts and the ultimate measures of their success.

Human dignity recognizes the inherent worth and value of every individual, regardless of their gender identity or expression. This principle demands that institutions treat all community members with respect, honor their self-determination, and create conditions that allow them to flourish as full human beings. Dignity is not something that must be earned or proven, but rather a fundamental characteristic that institutions must recognize and protect.

Belonging encompasses the feeling of being valued, accepted, and integral to a community. Unlike simple inclusion, which may involve being present without being truly welcomed, belonging involves experiencing genuine connection, mutual respect, and shared investment in collective success. For gender-expansive individuals, belonging often requires not only the absence of discrimination but the presence of affirmation, understanding, and celebration of their identities and contributions.

The relationship between dignity and belonging is reciprocal and reinforcing. When institutions honor the dignity of gender-expansive community members through respectful policies and practices, they create conditions for belonging. When individuals experience genuine belonging, their dignity is affirmed and their capacity to contribute to institutional mission is enhanced.

Working Towards Genuine Transformation

This chapter provides the conceptual foundation necessary to understand why gender inclusion requires more than policy adjustments or awareness training. By grounding implementation efforts in sophisticated understanding of gender identity and expression, intersectionality, transformative change, cultural competency, continuous improvement, community engagement, and human dignity, institutions can move beyond superficial compliance toward genuine transformation.

This framework challenges institutions to examine fundamental assumptions about gender that permeate organizational culture and operations while providing practical guidance for creating environments where all community members can thrive. It recognizes that this transformation requires sustained commitment, ongoing learning, and genuine partnership with gender-expansive communities.

STANDARD 3
ADMISSIONS PRACTICES AND CULTURE

THESE STANDARDS ENSURE that admissions and recruitment processes actively affirm and support gender diversity. From online applications and printed materials to campus visits and personal interactions, every step is designed to use inclusive language, respect chosen names and pronouns, and provide options beyond the gender binary. Leadership models inclusive behavior and prioritizes ongoing staff training to maintain awareness and accountability.

Continuous assessment and collaboration with campus and community partners support ongoing improvement. The goal is to create a welcoming, respectful experience that values all gender identities and sets the foundation for student success from the first point of contact.

3.A. Electronic Transactions

This category ensures that all digital components of the admissions process actively promote gender inclusivity. Online forms extend beyond traditional male/female options to include diverse gender identities and allow applicants to self-identify. Pronouns are collected optionally to respect individual preferences. The institution's website and applicant portals use gender-neutral language and enable chosen names to be used in communications, fostering an affirming and accessible experience. Search functions and digital content are designed to be inclusive and welcoming, regularly reviewed to maintain these standards.

> 3.A.1 All online forms include gender-inclusive options beyond the binary choice of "male" and "female," with options for self-identification.
> 3.A.2 Pronouns are collected as an optional field on all electronic application materials and portals.
> 3.A.3 Website content includes language that explicitly welcomes people of all genders (e.g., "people of all genders" rather than "men and women").
> 3.A.4 The institution's online portal allows applicants to specify their chosen name separate from legal name, with chosen names displayed in all relevant communication platforms.
> 3.A.5 Website search functionality includes terms related to transgender and nonbinary identities to improve information accessibility.
> 3.A.6 Electronic communications and digital marketing materials avoid gendered language, using "first-year students" rather than "freshmen," for example.

B. Print and Personal Communications

Print materials such as viewbooks, brochures, and recruitment forms reflect authentic gender diversity through inclusive language and imagery that avoids stereotypes. These materials provide options for applicants to indicate chosen names and pronouns, ensuring respectful representation. Admissions staff are trained to use gender-neutral language in conversations and written communications, honoring applicants' identities in all interactions. Staff wear pronoun badges, follow inclusive phone and greeting protocols, and are prepared to address misgendering sensitively, creating a welcoming and affirming recruitment environment.

> 3.B.1 Viewbooks, brochures, and recruitment materials feature diverse images that represent gender diversity and intersectionality.
> 3.B.2 Printed forms include gender-inclusive options beyond binary choices, with space for self-identification.
> 3.B.3 All print materials use gender-inclusive language (e.g., "they" as a singular pronoun when gender is unknown or irrelevant).

3.B.4 Publications like alum magazines and newsletters represent the achievements of individuals of all gender identities.

3.B.5 Campus maps clearly indicate the locations of gender-neutral restrooms and other gender-inclusive facilities.

3.B.6 Printed applications and other forms allow for chosen name in addition to legal name.

3.B.7 Design elements in print materials avoid color schemes and graphics that reinforce gender stereotypes.

3.B.8 Admissions staff use gender-neutral language when speaking with prospective students unless given specific information about a student's gender identity.

3.B.9 Name tags for admissions staff typically include pronouns, normalizing this practice.

3.B.10 Admissions staff honors students' chosen names and pronouns in all interactions.

3.B.11 Phone scripts and in-person greeting protocols avoid gendered language (e.g., "Welcome to our campus" rather than "Welcome, ladies and gentlemen").

3.B.12 Admissions interviews include space for applicants to share their pronouns if they choose.

C. Campus Visits and Tours

Campus visit experiences incorporate gender inclusivity through language and logistics. Tour scripts avoid gendered assumptions, and virtual tours highlight gender diversity among students and staff. Facilities such as gender-neutral restrooms and gender-inclusive housing options are emphasized. Policies support the needs of transgender and nonbinary students during overnight stays. Tour guides and student ambassadors receive training on gender diversity, and materials highlight resources like LGBTQIA+ centers and inclusive student organizations. Activities and group formations are designed to avoid gender-based divisions, ensuring all prospective students feel valued and included.

3.C.1 Campus tour scripts use gender-inclusive language throughout the experience.

3.C.2 Virtual tours and orientation videos represent gender diversity among students, faculty, and staff.

3.C.3 Tour routes include gender-neutral restrooms and highlight gender-inclusive housing options.

3.C.4 Overnight visit programs have policies that accommodate transgender and nonbinary students in ways that affirm their gender identities.

3.C.5 Campus visit registration forms allow prospective students to share their gender identity and pronouns if they choose.

3.C.6 Student ambassadors and tour guides receive training on gender diversity and inclusive language.

3.C.7 Information sessions avoid gendered statistics (e.g., rather than "40% of our students are male," say "our community includes students of all genders").

3.C.8 Campus visit materials highlight resources such as LGBTQIA+ centers, student organizations, and gender-inclusive housing.

3.C.9 Visitation day programs include options for prospective students to connect with LGBTQIA+ student organizations if desired.

3.C.10 Signage used during campus visit events uses gender-inclusive language.

3.C.11 Tour group formation and activities avoid gender-based divisions or assumptions.

D. Application Review Process (4-Year Selective Entry Colleges and Universities)

The admissions review process is structured to mitigate gender bias and promote equity. Rubrics recognize diverse expressions of leadership and achievement across gender identities. Committees include trained members who use respectful, gender-inclusive language and are mindful of unconscious biases. Application materials, including essays and recommendations, are evaluated with awareness of potential gender bias or misgendering. The process accommodates name and gender marker changes without penalty. Holistic review practices value gender diversity as an asset that enriches the campus community, while data on admission rates by gender identity are regularly examined to identify disparities.

3.D.1 Rubrics for application evaluation incorporate inclusive criteria that recognize diverse expressions of leadership, achievement, and experience across gender identities.

3.D.2 Application review committees include individuals with training in gender diversity and unconscious bias.

3.D.3 Discussion protocols during application review meetings establish norms for gender-inclusive language and respectful dialogue about applicants.

3.D.4 Reader training for application reviewers includes specific modules on avoiding gender bias in the evaluation of essays, activities, and recommendations.

3.D.5 The admissions committee regularly examines demographic patterns in admission rates across gender identities to identify and address potential disparities.

3.D.6 Standardized test score interpretation considers research on gender-based testing biases when contextualizing results.

3.D.7 Application review discussions avoid gender-based assumptions about academic interests, extracurricular activities, or career aspirations.

3.D.8 Letters of recommendation containing gender bias or misgendering language are evaluated with an awareness of how such language may misrepresent the applicant.

3.D.9 The review process accommodates name changes and gender marker updates that may occur during the application cycle without penalty to the applicant.

3.D.10 Holistic review practices value diverse experiences related to gender identity as potential contributions to campus diversity and perspective.

E. Training, Professional Development, and Knowledge Building

Ongoing education is central to maintaining a gender-inclusive admissions office. New hires undergo comprehensive training on gender diversity and inclusive language. Annual trainings keep staff updated on evolving terminology and best practices. Resources like libraries and professional development opportunities are made available to support knowledge growth. Reflective practices encourage staff to examine personal biases and socialization around gender, helping them engage more thoughtfully and effectively with diverse applicants.

3.E.1 The admissions office maintains a regularly updated resource library on gender diversity in higher education that is accessible to all staff.

3.E.2 New employee onboarding includes comprehensive training on gender diversity, inclusive language, and the office's gender-inclusive standards.

3.E.3 All admissions staff receive annual training on gender identity, pronouns, and appropriate terminology.

3.E.4 Staff meetings incorporate ongoing education about evolving terminology, practices, and considerations regarding gender identity.

3.E.5 The office culture encourages staff to attend conferences and webinars focused on supporting trans and gender-expansive students in higher education.

3.E.6 Admissions professionals engage in reflective practice regarding their own gender socialization and biases that may impact their work.

F. Leadership Values and High Impact Practices

Admissions leadership plays a key role in fostering a culture of gender inclusivity by modeling respectful behavior, including the use of correct pronouns and inclusive language. Leaders recognize and celebrate staff contributions toward these goals, embed gender diversity into hiring practices, and include inclusivity metrics in performance evaluations. Clear accountability measures address misgendering and insensitivity. Leadership commitment ensures the office environment prioritizes respect for all gender identities and drives ongoing progress in inclusivity initiatives.

3.F.1 The admissions leadership team models inclusive behavior by using correct pronouns, gender-inclusive language, and demonstrating respect for all gender identities.

3.F.2 Leaders actively celebrate and recognize staff contributions to creating a more gender-inclusive admissions environment.

3.F.3 Hiring practices for the admissions team prioritize diversity of lived experiences, including gender diversity among staff members.

3.F.4 Performance evaluations for admissions staff include metrics related to advancing gender inclusivity initiatives and high-impact practices.

3.F.5 Leaders establish clear accountability protocols for addressing instances of misgendering or gender-based insensitivity within the office.

G. Internal Communications

The office culture supports inclusivity through daily use of gender-neutral language in emails, meetings, and documents. Pronoun sharing is normalized but voluntary, creating a respectful environment for all. Visual cues such as pride flags and inclusive posters reinforce this culture physically. Staff members are encouraged to gently correct one another to reduce unnecessary gendered language, fostering continuous awareness and practice of inclusivity within the team.

3.G.1 Employee email signatures typically include pronouns to normalize this practice throughout the admissions process.

3.G.2 Internal communications and documents use gender-inclusive language consistently.

3.G.3 Employee meetings begin with pronoun introductions for visitors while maintaining a culture where sharing pronouns is invited but not required.

3.G.4 The office physical environment displays visual cues of gender inclusivity, such as pride flags, pronoun pins, or inclusive posters.

3.G.5 Gender-inclusive language is integrated into everyday conversation, with colleagues respectfully correcting one another when gendered terms are unnecessarily used.

H. Work Environment and Culture

The physical and social environment within the admissions office is intentionally designed to respect gender diversity. Facilities include all-gender restrooms accessible to staff and visitors. Social events avoid reinforcing gender binaries or stereotypes. Staff are empowered to address microaggressions and errors related to gender identity in a supportive manner that focuses on learning rather than blame. Privacy regarding personal gender information is carefully respected, creating a safe and respectful workplace for everyone.

3.H.1 The physical office space includes all gender restroom facilities accessible to staff and visitors.

3.H.2 Office events and social gatherings are planned with attention to gender inclusivity, avoiding activities that reinforce gender stereotypes or binary divisions.

3.H.3 Staff are empowered to respectfully address microaggressions related to gender identity when they occur in the workplace.

3.H.4 The office culture emphasizes learning from mistakes rather than shame when unintentional misgendering or other errors occur.

3.H.5 A culture of respect for privacy exists regarding personal information about gender identity for staff, visitors, and applicants.

I. Community Engagement and Representation

Admissions actively partners with campus LGBTQIA+ centers, student organizations, and external groups supporting transgender and gender-expansive youth to enhance recruitment and outreach. Alumni from diverse gender backgrounds participate in events, providing visible representation and encouragement to prospective students. The admissions office advocates for broader campus initiatives that improve gender inclusivity and ensure that prospective students encounter a welcoming and supportive environment beyond the admissions process.

> 3.I.1 The admissions team builds partnerships with campus LGBTQIA+ centers and student organizations to strengthen gender-inclusive recruitment efforts.
> 3.I.2 Staff participate in community events that demonstrate the institution's commitment to gender diversity and inclusion.
> 3.I.3 Alums from diverse gender backgrounds are engaged in recruitment activities and admissions events to reflect institutional inclusivity.
> 3.I.4 The admissions office collaborates with local and national organizations dedicated to supporting transgender and gender-expansive youth.
> 3.I.5 The admissions team advocates for gender-inclusive improvements across campus that impact prospective students' experiences.

J. Assessment and Growth

A commitment to continuous improvement guides the admissions office's gender inclusivity efforts. Regular cultural assessments and gender equity audits of materials help identify areas for growth. Feedback from transgender and gender-expansive applicants, students, and staff informs practices and policies. The office tracks metrics to evaluate the impact of inclusivity initiatives on application and enrollment outcomes. A dedicated staff member or committee ensures that gender-inclusive policies are reviewed and updated annually. Celebrating successes while acknowledging ongoing challenges fosters a culture of accountability and progress.

> 3.J.1 Regular cultural assessments within the admissions office identify areas for growth in gender inclusivity practices.

3.J.2 The office culture embraces evolving best practices in gender inclusivity rather than maintaining the status quo.

3.J.3 All print materials undergo a gender equity audit to ensure proportional, authentic representation of individuals across the gender spectrum.

3.J.4 Feedback from transgender and gender-expansive applicants, students, and staff is valued and incorporated into high-impact practices.

3.J.5 The admissions team celebrates progress in creating a more gender-inclusive environment while acknowledging ongoing opportunities for improvement.

3.J.6 Metrics are established to monitor the impact of gender-inclusive practices on application and yield rates among diverse gender identities.

3.J.7 A dedicated staff member or committee is responsible for reviewing and updating gender-inclusive policies annually.

3.J.8 The Admissions Office conducts an annual audit of all materials and procedures to ensure gender inclusivity.

STANDARD 4
CURRICULUM AND PEDAGOGY

INCLUSIVE CURRICULUM and Pedagogy Standards aim to create equitable and supportive educational environments for all students, including transgender and gender-expansive individuals. These standards focus on integrating diverse gender perspectives into academic content, teaching practices, faculty development, classroom environments, and continuous improvement measures. Overall, these standards ensure that gender diversity is meaningfully incorporated into higher education, benefiting all students by promoting inclusivity, respect, and equal opportunity. They reflect a commitment to not only addressing gender diversity in course content but also creating teaching practices and classroom environments that actively support and value transgender and gender-expansive students.

A. Curricular Content

These standards are essential for ensuring that course materials, readings, case studies, and examples reflect a broad range of gender experiences, including those of transgender and gender-expansive scholars. By incorporating gender diversity into both core courses and specialized offerings, academic departments can provide students with a more comprehensive understanding of the world and prepare them for inclusive and diverse professional environments. Gender-inclusive language and catalog designations further facilitate access to these important courses, enhancing visibility and representation throughout the curriculum.

4.A.1 Academic departments conduct regular curriculum reviews to ensure diverse gender representations and perspectives are meaningfully integrated into course materials.

4.A.2 Course materials (readings, case studies, examples) include works by transgender and gender-expansive scholars and represent diverse gender experiences across disciplines.

4.A.3 Academic programs offer at least one course specifically focused on gender diversity, or substantially incorporate gender diversity within existing courses.

4.A.4 Course catalogs include a searchable designation for courses that substantially address gender diversity topics.

4.A.5 Language in all syllabi and course descriptions is gender-inclusive and avoids binary assumptions.

B. Pedagogical Practice

Advancing pedagogical practices fosters an inclusive classroom atmosphere where students' identities are respected. By encouraging the use of pronouns, avoiding binary assumptions, and integrating inclusive practices like using students' chosen names and pronouns, faculty contribute to a safe and welcoming learning environment.

4.B.1 Faculty employ inclusive classroom practices (both online and face-to-face), including using students' chosen names and pronouns, avoiding gender-segregated activities, and using gender-inclusive language.

4.B.2 All faculty include pronouns on syllabi and encourage (but never require) students to share pronouns if comfortable doing so.

4.B.3 Syllabi include statements of inclusion that specifically acknowledge gender diversity and establish classroom expectations for respectful engagement.

4.B.4 Course evaluations include questions assessing the extent to which courses create inclusive learning environments for transgender and gender-expansive students.

C. Faculty Development

These standards ensure that all faculty receive foundational training on gender-inclusive teaching practices. Ongoing professional development opportunities support continuous learning and adaptation to new practices, ensuring that teaching methods remain inclusive and effective. Faculty are also encouraged to collaborate and share strategies for fostering inclusive classrooms, which improves teaching quality and also strengthens the institutional commitment to gender diversity.

> 4.C.1 Faculty participate in foundational professional development on gender-inclusive teaching practices within their first year.
> 4.C.2 Ongoing professional development opportunities on gender-inclusive teaching are regularly available to all instructional staff.
> 4.C.3 Teaching and learning centers provide resources, consultations, and workshops focused specifically on gender inclusion in the classroom.
> 4.C.4 Departments foster communities of practice where faculty can share strategies for creating gender-inclusive learning environments.
> 4.C.5 Faculty evaluation and promotion processes recognize and reward efforts to create inclusive learning environments.

D. Classroom Environment

Classroom environment standards emphasize the importance of creating a classroom climate where gender-related discussions can take place respectfully, without burdening transgender or gender-expansive students. Clear protocols for addressing misgendering and bias, as well as the use of Universal Design for Learning, ensure that all students, regardless of gender identity, can access and engage with the curriculum. Faculty also foster inclusivity by soliciting ongoing feedback from students about classroom climate, allowing for timely adjustments to maintain an open and respectful environment.

> 4.D.1 Classroom discussions about gender-related topics are facilitated in ways that don't tokenize or place undue burden on transgender or gender-expansive students.
> 4.D.2 Faculty establish clear protocols for addressing instances of misgendering or bias in the classroom.
> 4.D.3 Faculty employ Universal Design for Learning principles to create accessible learning environments for all students, including considerations for gender-expansive students.

4.D.4 Multiple forms of participation and assessment are offered to accommodate different learning styles and comfort levels.

4.D.5 Faculty create opportunities for student feedback on classroom climate throughout the term, not just in end-of-course evaluations.

E. Assessment and Continuous Improvement

These standards help institutions evaluate the success of their gender-inclusive practices by gathering data on student outcomes, such as course completion and major selection, specifically for transgender and gender-expansive students. By regularly assessing whether these students feel supported across the curriculum, departments can identify and address potential barriers to success. The process of sharing teaching innovations and student feedback helps institutions continuously improve their inclusivity, ensuring long-term progress and adaptation.

4.E.1 Institutions collect disaggregated data on course completion, major selection, and academic success for transgender and gender-expansive students to identify potential barriers.

4.E.2 Departments regularly assess whether gender-expansive students feel equally supported and engaged across the curriculum.

4.E.3 Curriculum committees include consideration of gender inclusion in the course approval process.

4.E.4 Teaching innovations related to gender inclusion are documented, assessed, and shared across the institution.

4.E.5 Students have accessible pathways to provide feedback on curriculum and pedagogy related to gender inclusion.

STANDARD 5
STUDENT LIFE AND CO-CURRICULAR ENGAGEMENT

STUDENT LIFE and co-curricular engagement are central to fostering a sense of belonging and personal growth in higher education. For transgender and gender-expansive students, inclusive practices in these areas can profoundly shape their experiences, safety, and overall well-being. This standard provides guidance for institutions to create environments where gender diversity is acknowledged, respected, and supported across all facets of campus life. From residential settings to student organizations, athletics, campus events, and support services, the following standards reflect a commitment to affirmation, equity, and accessibility. Staff development, professional training, and thoughtful program design help ensure that students' identities are recognized and supported in meaningful ways. Additionally, ongoing assessment and responsiveness to student feedback are essential to sustaining inclusive practices, allowing institutions to adapt and grow in alignment with the evolving needs of their transgender and gender-expansive communities.

A. Residence Life

Institutions are encouraged to offer gender-inclusive living and co-curricular environments without additional barriers. Staff training should center on affirming practices—respecting pronouns, ensuring privacy, and navigating relationship and conflict dynamics. Housing policies should align with students' gender identities and explicitly support diverse expressions of gender.

5.A.1 All new and returning students have access to gender-inclusive housing solutions that do not require additional documentation, medical information, or special approval processes.

5.A.2 Residence halls include all-gender bathrooms and shower facilities that are accessible, clearly marked, and available on every floor.

5.A.3 Housing assignment processes allow students to room with others based on their gender identity rather than sex assigned at birth.

5.A.4 Residence Life policies and roommate agreements explicitly address respect for gender identity and expression.

5.A.5. Residence or Community Assistants receive comprehensive training on supporting transgender and gender-expansive students.

B. Student Organizations and Leadership

Campus groups lead with inclusivity and belonging by embedding gender identity and expression into non-discrimination policies and ensuring equitable funding for LGBTQIA+ initiatives. Supporting the formation of affinity groups, incorporating gender inclusion into leadership training, and conducting regular climate assessments can foster a more representative and welcoming institution.

5.B.1 Student government and organization constitutions include non-discrimination clauses that specifically mention gender identity and expression.

5.B.2 Funding for student organizations is equitably distributed, with dedicated resources for LGBTQIA+ and gender-expansive student groups.

5.B.3 Gender-expansive students have opportunities to form affinity groups and community spaces specific to their identities and experiences.

5.B.4 Leadership development programs include content on creating inclusive organizations and addressing unconscious bias related to gender identity.

5.B.5 Student organizations undergo regular self-assessments to evaluate how well they support members of all gender identities.

C. Campus Activities and Events

Inclusive event planning should involve offering all-gender spaces, avoiding binary structures, and updating traditions to reflect gender diversity. Programming that celebrates gender-expansive identities and uses affirming language and imagery can help normalize inclusion as a campus-wide value.

> 5.C.1 Event registration processes allow for the indication of all-gender spaces, accessible bathrooms, and other inclusive accommodations.
> 5.C.2 Campus events avoid unnecessary gender segregation or binary gender expectations (e.g., in registration forms, activities, or recognition ceremonies).
> 5.C.3 Major campus traditions and ceremonies are regularly reviewed and modified to ensure they are inclusive of all gender identities.
> 5.C.4 Campus programming includes events specifically celebrating gender diversity (e.g., Transgender Day of Visibility, Pride Month).
> 5.C.5 Event marketing and promotional materials feature diverse gender representations and use inclusive language.

D. Athletics and Recreation

Athletics programs and recreational spaces should aim to include gender-neutral facilities and offer participation options beyond binary divisions. Fitness programs and staff training can reflect a commitment to welcoming all gender identities, grounded in awareness of policy and best practices.

> 5.D.1 Campus recreation facilities include gender-inclusive changing rooms and bathroom facilities that are easily accessible.
> 5.D.2 Recreation center policies explicitly protect the rights of transgender and gender-expansive students to participate in activities aligned with their gender identity.
> 5.D.3 Intramural and club sports offer gender-inclusive participation options beyond binary men's and women's teams.
> 5.D.4 Fitness classes and wellness programs are marketed and designed to be welcoming to people of all gender identities.

E. Support Services and Programming

Orientation, mentoring, and career services can be designed with gender expansive students in mind—from introducing inclusive resources to addressing name changes and workplace transitions. Ongoing, student-led programming and thoughtful assessment strategies can ensure that support remains responsive and relevant.

> 5.E.1 Virtual and face-to-face orientation programs include content introducing gender inclusion concepts and campus resources for transgender and gender-expansive students.
>
> 5.E.2 Peer mentoring programs include options specifically for transgender and gender-expansive students.
>
> 5.E.3 Campus programming regularly addresses topics related to gender identity, with leadership and participation from transgender and gender-expansive students.
>
> 5.E.4 Student life assessment efforts include specific measures to evaluate the experiences of transgender and gender-expansive students.

F. Training, Professional Development, and Knowledge Building

The following standards highlight the importance of equipping campus personnel with the knowledge and skills to support transgender and gender-expansive students effectively. Through comprehensive training across functional areas, staff are prepared to respond with respect, awareness, and sensitivity to the diverse needs of these students. This commitment fosters a more inclusive campus climate where belonging, safety, and equitable access are upheld.

> 5.F.1 Staff receive comprehensive training on supporting transgender and gender-expansive students, including pronoun usage, privacy considerations, and conflict resolution strategies.
>
> 5.F.2 Athletics staff receive training on supporting transgender and gender-expansive athletes, including athletic accreditation organizations and other relevant policy guidelines.
>
> 5.F.3 Career services staff are trained to support transgender and gender-expansive students with unique challenges related to professional development (name changes on resumes, interview preparation, clothing, workplace transitions).
>
> 5.F.4 Crisis response teams include members trained in the specific needs of transgender and gender-expansive students.

5.F.5 Campus safety officers receive specialized training on respectful interactions with transgender and gender-expansive students.

G. Crisis Response and Safety

Emergency procedures, bias reporting systems, and safety personnel training should reflect an understanding of the experiences of gender-expansive students. Accessible advocacy and informed crisis response can help build trust and ensure equitable treatment in moments of vulnerability.

5.G.1 Campus safety protocols include specific considerations for supporting transgender and gender-expansive students during emergencies.
5.G.2 Reporting mechanisms for bias incidents related to gender identity are clearly communicated and accessible.
5.G.3 Confidential advocacy services are available for transgender and gender-expansive students experiencing harassment or discrimination.

STANDARD 6
INTERSECTIONALITY

THIS STANDARD PROVIDES a comprehensive framework for advancing equity and inclusion for gender-expansive students whose experiences are shaped by multiple, intersecting identities. It emphasizes the importance of understanding how gender identity interacts with other dimensions of identity—such as race, ethnicity, socioeconomic status, disability, nationality, and more—to influence access, opportunity, and well-being. Institutions are encouraged to adopt policies, programs, and services that are responsive to this complexity, ensuring that all students are supported in ways that are both affirming and culturally aware. By embedding intersectional thinking into assessment, resource allocation, programming, training, healthcare, and advocacy, colleges and universities can proactively address systemic barriers, enhance student belonging, and foster inclusive communities where the full spectrum of gender diversity is recognized and valued. These standards highlight the need for ongoing engagement with students themselves, ensuring that initiatives reflect lived experiences and evolving needs, and that institutional practices are continually refined to promote equity across all dimensions of identity.

A. Recognition and Assessment

Institutions are encouraged to design data systems that honor the complexity of identity while protecting student privacy. Disaggregated climate data and intersectional assessment tools—developed with student input—can illuminate systemic gaps and inform equity efforts. Analyzing retention, engagement, and outcomes through an intersectional lens supports more targeted and responsive strategies.

> 6.A.1 Access to Institutional data collection tools and systems allow students to self-identify across multiple dimensions of identity while maintaining appropriate privacy protections.
>
> 6.A.2 Campus climate assessments disaggregate experiences of transgender and gender-expansive students by race, disability status, socioeconomic background, nationality, and other relevant identities.
>
> 6.A.3 Institutions regularly audit and assess services, programs, and policies to identify potential barriers affecting gender-expansive students with multiple marginalized identities.
>
> 6.A.4 Quantitative metrics on student entry, retention, graduation, and engagement are analyzed at the intersections of gender identity with other marginalized identities.
>
> 6.A.5 Assessment methodologies are designed with input from gender-expansive students with multiple marginalized identities.

B. Resource Allocation and Support

Financial aid, emergency funding, and scholarships should acknowledge the specific barriers faced by students who may be disconnected from family or support networks. Building partnerships with community organizations and fostering collaboration across campus resource centers can ensure more holistic, culturally responsive care for students with intersecting identities.

> 6.A.1 Financial aid processes recognize and address unique challenges faced by gender-expansive students who may lack family support.
>
> 6.A.2 Emergency funding is accessible to address the acute needs of gender-expansive students with multiple marginalized identities.
>
> 6.A.3 Scholarship and fellowship opportunities explicitly welcome applications from gender-expansive students with multiple marginalized identities.
>
> 6.A.4 Student support services establish and maintain referral relationships with community-based organizations serving specific intersectional populations (e.g., transgender people of color, transgender people with disabilities).

6.A.5 Campus resource centers collaborate across identity-focused offices (e.g., LGBTQIA+ center, multicultural center, international programs, disability services) to provide integrated support.

6.A.6 Campus resource centers and identity-focused offices recognize the unique challenges faced by international students coming from countries where LGBTQIA+ rights are restricted or prohibited.

6.A.7 Budget Development governance structures ensure consistent allocations to LGBTQIA+ students to advance student equity and success.

C. Programming and Community Building

Intentional programming should center the lived experiences of gender-expansive students at various intersections—across race, class, disability, nationality, and more. Affinity spaces, peer mentoring, and cross-community initiatives can foster a deeper sense of belonging and solidarity, while ensuring diverse voices are reflected in both content and leadership.

6.C.1 Campus programming consistently addresses and celebrates intersectional experiences within gender diversity through speakers, workshops, and educational events.

6.C.2 Affinity spaces exist and thrive for gender-expansive students with specific intersecting identities (e.g., transgender students of color, international transgender students).

6.C.3 Mentoring programs connect gender-expansive students with mentors who share multiple aspects of their identities when possible.

6.C.4 Community-building initiatives recognize and work towards fostering solidarity and understanding across different marginalized groups.

6.C.5 Programming about transgender and gender-expansive experiences consistently includes diverse representations across race, disability, class, religion, and other identity dimensions.

D. Training, Professional Development and Knowledge Building

Faculty, staff, and students benefit from training that explores how systems of power and privilege compound across identities. Curriculum development and leadership programs can intentionally lift up intersectional narratives, while anti-bias training should address the microaggressions that arise from overlapping forms of marginalization.

> 6.D.1 Training for faculty, staff, and student leaders addresses how systems of oppression interact and compound for gender-expansive people with multiple marginalized identities.
>
> 6.D.2 Educational materials on gender inclusion incorporate intersectional frameworks and avoid one-dimensional representations.
>
> 6.D.3 Curriculum development includes attention to intersectional gender-expansive perspectives across disciplines.
>
> 6.D.4 Leadership development programs prepare gender-expansive students with multiple marginalized identities for advocacy roles.
>
> 6.D.5 Faculty, staff and students recognize the ways that intersectional microaggressions can target multiple aspects of gender-expansive students' identities.

E. Healthcare and Wellness

Health and counseling services are encouraged to build capacity in serving gender-expansive students with complex, intersectional needs—whether related to trauma, access, or chronic health disparities. Inclusive coverage policies and health education materials should reflect diverse bodies and experiences across gender, race, ability, and economic status.

> 6.E.1 Healthcare providers receive specialized training on serving gender-expansive patients with intersecting identities such as race, disability, and socioeconomic status.
>
> 6.E.2 Mental health services include clinicians with expertise in addressing trauma related to multiple systems of oppression.
>
> 6.E.3 Wellness programs address health disparities affecting gender-expansive people from various marginalized communities.
>
> 6.E.4 Health insurance coverage accounts for the specific needs of gender-expansive students with disabilities, chronic conditions, hormone replacement therapy, or other health concerns.
>
> 6.E.5 Health education materials represent diverse bodies and experiences across gender, race, disability, and other identities.

F. Institutional Advocacy

Leadership can play a key role in dismantling structural inequities by reviewing policies through an intersectional lens and championing inclusive practices at all levels. Hiring for lived experience and expertise, amplifying intersectional voices in communications, and embedding these priorities into strategic DEI planning all signal a sustained institutional commitment.

> 6.F.1 Campus leadership actively addresses policies that disproportionately impact gender-expansive students with multiple marginalized identities.
>
> 6.F.2 Institutional advocacy efforts on behalf of gender-expansive students extend to state and national levels, particularly for issues affecting those with multiple marginalized identities.
>
> 6.F.3 Hiring practices prioritize recruiting staff and faculty who have lived experience and/or expertise working with intersectional gender diversity.
>
> 6.F.4 Public communications about gender inclusion consistently incorporate intersectional perspectives.
>
> 6.F.5 Strategic plans for diversity, equity, and inclusion specifically address the needs of gender-expansive students with multiple marginalized identities.

STANDARD 7
RECRUITING AND RETAINING GENDER-EXPANSIVE EMPLOYEES

THIS STANDARD PROVIDES a strategic framework for fostering equitable participation, advancement, and well-being for transgender and gender-expansive employees. It encourages institutions to build intentional systems that attract diverse talent, ensure fair and consistent treatment, and cultivate inclusive workplace cultures. By embedding gender inclusion into recruitment, onboarding, benefits, professional development, workplace climate, and accountability structures, institutions can create environments where gender-expansive employees are supported, valued, and empowered to thrive. This framework emphasizes not only structural policies but also cultural and interpersonal practices, recognizing that meaningful inclusion requires attention to both the formal systems of employment and the everyday experiences of staff and faculty. Leadership commitment, ongoing training, mentorship, and visible advocacy are essential to sustain progress and normalize gender diversity as a core aspect of institutional excellence.

A. Recruitment and Hiring

Job postings and outreach efforts should reflect an demonstrated explicit commitment to gender diversity, supported by search processes that include trained diversity advocates and anti-bias education. Institutions may benefit from building relationships with gender-expansive professional networks and showcasing visible inclusion across recruitment materials.

7.A.1 Job postings explicitly state the institution's commitment to gender diversity and inclusion, including specific language welcoming applications from transgender and gender-expansive applicants and candidates.

7.A.2 Search committees receive comprehensive training on recognizing and mitigating implicit bias related to gender identity and expression.

7.A.3 Hiring processes include diversity advocates who are specifically trained to ensure gender-inclusive frameworks and practices throughout the search.

7.A.4 Recruitment materials feature visible representation of gender diversity and highlight institutional support for transgender and gender-expansive employees.

7.A.5 Professional networks and outreach efforts specifically target transgender and gender-expansive communities, including specialized job boards and professional associations.

B. Onboarding and Integration

Welcoming environments begin with orientation processes that affirm chosen names, pronouns, and identities. Institutions can strengthen inclusion by connecting new hires with mentors and affinity groups, providing clear guidance on gender-inclusive policies, and ensuring supervisors are prepared to support gender-expansive employees.

7.B.1 Institutional forms and systems allow employees to indicate chosen names, pronouns, and gender identities with clear protocols for updating these as needed.

7.B.2 New faculty and staff are connected with mentors and affinity groups that can support their integration into the campus community.

7.B.3 Onboarding materials include information about gender-inclusive policies, practices, and resources, including healthcare benefits..

7.B.4 Administrative systems and ID cards use employees' chosen names and accurate gender markers.

7.B.5 Department chairs and supervisors receive guidance on creating welcoming environments for transgender and gender-expansive employees.

C. Benefits and Compensation

Comprehensive benefits should include gender-affirming healthcare and leave options that support transition-related needs. Institutions are encouraged to recognize nontraditional family structures in policy design and conduct regular equity reviews to identify pay disparities related to gender identity.

> 7.C.1 Health insurance policies for employees cover gender-affirming care including hormone therapy, surgical procedures, and related mental health services without exclusions.
>
> 7.C.2 Leave policies accommodate gender transition-related needs, including recovery from medical procedures.
>
> 7.C.3 Employee assistance programs include providers with expertise in supporting transgender and gender-expansive individuals.
>
> 7.C.4 Family benefits recognize diverse family structures and definitions beyond cisgender and heteronormative models.
>
> 7.C.5 Regular equity analyses of compensation include gender identity as a factor to identify and address any pay disparities.

D. Training, Professional Development and Knowledge Building

Promotion processes and performance evaluations and advancement should acknowledge the unique contributions of gender-expansive faculty and staff, especially in areas like mentorship and diversity-related service. Dedicated leadership pathways and institutional funding for gender-focused scholarship can support long-term advancement and visibility.

> 7.D.1 Performance evaluation frameworks value diversity-related service and mentoring work, which often falls disproportionately on faculty from marginalized groups.
>
> 7.D.2 Professional development opportunities include specific support for transgender and gender-expansive employees' career advancement–both inside and outside of the institution.
>
> 7.D.3 Tenure and promotion committees receive training on recognizing and mitigating bias against transgender and gender-expansive faculty.

7.D.4 Leadership development programs actively recruit and support gender-expansive participants.

7.D.5 Institutional funding supports research, teaching, and service work related to gender diversity and transgender studies.

E. Workplace Climate

A gender-inclusive workplace might include accessible restrooms, respectful communication standards, and administrative systems that reflect employees' lived identities. Dress codes should avoid binary expectations. Climate assessments can help track and improve the daily experiences of gender-expansive employees.

7.E.1 All workplace facilities include accessible gender-neutral restrooms and changing spaces.

7.E.2 Institutional communication standards use gender-inclusive language in all documents, web content, and official correspondence.

7.E.3 Regular climate assessments measure the experiences of transgender and gender-expansive employees with data disaggregated by position type.

7.E.4 Dress codes and appearance policies respect gender diversity and avoid binary or stereotypical expectations.

F. Support and Community

Institutions can foster belonging through affinity spaces, allyship training, and visible leadership support. Confidential resources should be available for employees navigating workplace challenges, and public institutional responses to anti-transgender events or legislation should demonstrate clear solidarity.

7.F.1 Employee resource groups or affinity spaces exist for transgender and gender-expansive employees with institutional support.

7.F.2 Institutional leadership visibly supports transgender and gender-expansive employees through public statements, participation in relevant events, and policy advocacy.

7.F.3 Ally programs train cisgender employees to effectively support their transgender and gender-expansive colleagues.

7.F.4 Confidential resources exist for transgender and gender-expansive employees to address workplace concerns or challenges.

7.F.5 Institutional responses to anti-transgender legislation or incidents clearly demonstrate support for gender-expansive community members.

G. Policy and Accountability

Robust protections for gender identity and expression should be embedded in non-discrimination policies, with clear procedures for enforcement. Transition support, name/gender change processes, and targeted bias reporting protocols help create environments where gender-expansive employees are respected and protected. Leadership accountability for inclusion efforts is key to sustained progress.

7.G.1 Non-discrimination policies and procedures explicitly protect gender identity and expression, with clear enforcement mechanisms.

7.G.2 Transition support guidelines outline institutional resources and processes for employees undergoing gender transition.

7.G.3 Name and gender marker change processes are simple, accessible, and do not require medical documentation.

7.G.4 Bias incident reporting systems include specialized protocols for addressing incidents related to gender identity and expression.

7.G.5 Leadership performance evaluations include metrics related to creating inclusive environments for transgender and gender-expansive employees.

STANDARD 8
INSTITUTIONAL POLICIES AND PRACTICES

THIS STANDARD OFFERS a comprehensive framework for cultivating campuses where transgender and gender-expansive individuals are not merely accommodated but fully affirmed and empowered to thrive. It emphasizes the integration of gender inclusion into every aspect of institutional operations—governance, policy, infrastructure, record-keeping, and culture—while prioritizing clarity, care, and accountability. Institutions are encouraged to create administrative systems, such as those managed by registrars, that respect chosen names, pronouns, and gender markers consistently across all records and communications, and allow for easy, confidential updates without unnecessary documentation. Beyond administrative compliance, the framework emphasizes proactive cultural and structural measures, including inclusive facilities, equitable policies, and responsive grievance processes. Leadership commitment, strategic planning, and community engagement are central, ensuring that gender inclusiveness is embedded in both decision-making and daily campus life, fostering an environment where gender-expansive students, staff, and faculty can fully participate and flourish.

A. Non-Discrimination & Equal Opportunity

Colleges and universities must enshrine protections for gender identity, expression, and transgender status within their official non-discrimination policies. These protections should be visible in equal opportunity statements on websites, job postings, and other institutional communications. Safeguards must apply across the entire campus ecosystem—

including housing, athletics, admissions, and employment—as well as to all contractors and affiliates. Regular policy reviews ensure institutions remain aligned with evolving language and best practices in gender equity.

> 8.A.1 Institutional non-discrimination policies and procedures explicitly include "gender identity," "gender expression," and "transgender status" as protected categories, and in accordance with state and federal laws.
>
> 8.A.2 Equal opportunity statements appear on all major institutional communications and websites with specific mention of gender identity and expression.
>
> 8.A.3 Policies and procedures explicitly prohibit discrimination based on gender identity in all aspects of academic and campus life, including admissions, housing, athletics, and employment.
>
> 8.A.4 Gender identity protections extend to all institutional partners, vendors, and contracted services.
>
> 8.A.5 Non-discrimination policies and procedures are regularly reviewed and updated to reflect evolving language and understanding of gender diversity.

B. Name, Gender Marker & Records

Institutional systems must respect and reflect chosen names, pronouns, and gender identities across all platforms—from class rosters and email systems to diplomas and payroll. Updates to personal information should be accessible through a simple process that does not require medical documentation. Strong privacy protocols must limit who can access information about previous names or gender markers. Alumni must be able to retroactively update credentials, while current records maintain consistency between internal accuracy and public affirmation.

> 8.B.1 Institutional systems allow students and employees to indicate and update gender markers and chosen names, and gender identities, through a simple administrative process that does not require medical or legal documentation, and which automatically populates across all internal systems.
>
> 8.B.2 Privacy protocols protect information about gender identity and previous names, with clear limitations on who can access this information and under what circumstances.
>
> 8.B.3 Admissions and records information, including diploma, transcript, and

credential policies, allow for retroactive updating of documents to reflect current names for alums.

8.B.4 Record-keeping systems maintain accurate historical records while respecting current identities in all public-facing documentation.

C. Grievance & Resolution Processes

Reporting pathways for bias, harassment, or discrimination must be inclusive, transparent, and easy to navigate. These processes should explicitly address gender identity and expression, offering multiple channels—including anonymous options—for individuals to seek support. Investigators and Title IX staff must be trained to handle gender-expansive cases with competence and care. Resolution models should aim to foster learning and restoration alongside accountability, especially in cases of bias or misunderstanding.

8.C.1 Bias response protocols and practices specifically address incidents related to gender identity and expression.

8.C.2 Multiple reporting channels exist for individuals experiencing harassment or discrimination based on gender identity.

8.C.3 Title IX coordinator, offices, and investigators receive specialized training on addressing complaints involving transgender and gender-expansive individuals.

8.C.4 Resolution processes prioritize educational outcomes and restorative approaches when addressing incidents of bias or misunderstanding.

8.C.5 Anonymous reporting mechanisms exist for individuals who fear retaliation for reporting gender-based discrimination.

D. Facilities & Infrastructure

All-gender restrooms and changing areas must be standard across campuses, including in both new buildings and renovation plans. Campus maps and signage should make these facilities easy to find and clearly labeled—free from stigmatizing imagery or language. Infrastructure audits must prioritize accessibility for transgender individuals, particularly those with intersecting needs, such as disability. Physical space reflects cultural values—gender-inclusive design must be a baseline, not a bonus.

8.D.1 Campus master plans include provisions to create or convert single-occupancy restrooms into gender-neutral facilities in all campus buildings.

8.D.2 New construction and renovation projects automatically incorporate gender-inclusive restrooms, locker rooms, and other gender-inclusive facilities.

8.D.3 Signage for all-gender facilities is clear, consistent, and free from potentially stigmatizing imagery.

8.D.4 Facility accessibility audits consider the needs of transgender and gender-expansive individuals, especially those with disabilities.

8.D.5 Gender-inclusive facilities are included in campus maps and wayfinding systems.

E. Data Collection & Assessment

Institutions must adopt inclusive data practices that reflect the full range of gender identities beyond the binary. This data should be collected thoughtfully and used to inform climate assessments, equity strategies, and institutional decision-making. Privacy must be rigorously protected, with clear protocols for how gender data is gathered, stored, and shared. Ongoing tracking and analysis help measure progress and guide improvements in programming, services, and policy.

8.E.1 Institutional research offices collect gender identity data using inclusive categories that go beyond binary options.

8.E.2 Privacy protocols govern how gender identity data is collected, stored, and used in institutional research.

8.E.3 Assessment instruments and program evaluations include questions about inclusivity for transgender and gender-expansive individuals.

8.E.4 Data about the experiences of transgender and gender-expansive community members is regularly reported to senior leadership and used for decision-making.

8.E.5 Longitudinal tracking measures progress on gender inclusion metrics over time.

8.E.6 Reports using gender identity data avoid practices that might inadvertently reveal individual identities in small populations.

F. Policy Development & Review

All policy work should center gender inclusion from the start, incorporating feedback from transgender and gender-expansive community members throughout the development and revision process. Regular audits of existing policies ensure language is inclusive and impacts are equitable. Institutions should conduct gender impact assessments for major initiatives and prioritize changes to policies that disproportionately harm gender-expansive individuals. Oversight from a standing inclusion advisory group ensures accountability and momentum.

> 8.F.1 Policy development processes include meaningful consultation with transgender and gender-expansive community members.
>
> 8.F.2 All institutional policies and procedures undergo regular review for gender-inclusive language and assumptions.
>
> 8.F.3 Gender impact assessments are conducted for new policies, procedures, and major initiatives to identify potential unintended consequences.
>
> 8.F.4 Policy and procedure revision processes prioritize addressing policies and procedures that disproportionately affect transgender and gender-expansive individuals.
>
> 8.F.5 A board-appointed standing committee or advisory group focused on gender inclusion reviews and recommends policy changes.

G. Leadership & Governance

Institutional leadership must embed gender equity into strategic priorities, budget planning, and evaluation frameworks. Representation of transgender and gender-expansive individuals within advisory boards and governance structures is essential to inclusive decision-making. Leadership evaluations should include measurable inclusion metrics, and public commitments must be backed by ongoing communication and visible action. Inclusion isn't an initiative—it's a leadership responsibility. Diversity, equity, and inclusion plans explicitly address goals related to gender inclusion with measurable outcomes.

> 8.G.1 Budget allocations support initiatives advancing gender inclusion across the institution.
>
> 8.G.2 Leadership teams and the board of trustees regularly participate in training

and professional development regarding transgender and gender-expansive students and employees.

8.G.3 Leadership performance evaluations include metrics related to advancing gender inclusion.

8.G.4 Transgender and gender-expansive individuals are represented in governance bodies and advisory committees.

8.G.5 Senior leadership regularly communicates institutional commitments to gender inclusion and progress on related initiatives.

H. External Engagement & Advocacy

Institutions should extend their gender equity values beyond the campus gates. This includes advocating for supportive legislation, taking public stances against anti-trans policies, and showcasing inclusion in donor relations, alum outreach, and communications. External requests for gender-related data must be handled transparently and in collaboration with impacted communities. Through bold, values-driven advocacy, institutions can help shift the broader landscape toward justice.

8.H.1 Institutional government relations efforts advocate for transgender-supportive policies at local, state, and federal levels.

8.H.2 Public statements opposing anti-transgender legislation are issued when relevant to the institution's community.

8.H.3 Donor and alum relations emphasize the institution's commitment to gender inclusion.

8.H.4 External communications highlight the institution's gender-inclusive practices and accomplishments.

8.H.5 Institutional responses to external requests for gender-related data and information are developed in consultation with gender-expansive community members.

STANDARD 9
CAMPUS SPACES

THIS STANDARD PROVIDES guidance for creating campuses that are genuinely welcoming, accessible, and affirming for all students, regardless of their gender identity or expression. Institutions are encouraged to approach space design, infrastructure, and wayfinding with the understanding that transgender and gender-expansive students experience environments differently, and that inclusion requires thoughtful attention to both privacy and visibility. From restrooms and changing areas to residential housing, learning spaces, health facilities, and social gathering spots, every space should reflect respect for diverse identities and offer flexible, safe, and supportive options. Signage, maps, digital tools, and symbolic representations—from public art to student displays—should reinforce gender inclusivity and celebrate contributions from transgender and gender-expansive communities. Safety, privacy, and accessibility must be prioritized, ensuring that physical spaces and campus navigation systems allow all students to move freely, confidently, and securely. By embedding these principles across both formal and informal campus spaces, institutions demonstrate a commitment to an environment where gender-expansive students are fully acknowledged, respected, and able to thrive socially, academically, and personally.

A. Restroom & Changing Facilities

Campus buildings should include at least one ADA-compliant, all-gender restroom on each floor or within reasonable proximity. Recreation, athletic, and aquatic centers must provide private, accessible changing and shower facilities for individuals of all gender identities. New construction and renovations should incorporate multiple all-gender restrooms as a default. Wayfinding tools like maps and mobile apps should clearly identify the locations of these facilities. Signage must use inclusive language and imagery that moves beyond the gender binary.

> 9.A.1 All campus buildings include at least one clearly marked, ADA-accessible all-gender restroom on every floor or within a reasonable distance.
> 9.A.2 Recreation centers, athletic facilities, and aquatic centers include private changing areas and shower facilities accessible to people of all gender identities.
> 9.A.3 All new construction and major renovation projects incorporate multiple all-gender restrooms by default.
> 9.A.4 Signage for all-gender facilities uses inclusive terminology and imagery that avoids reinforcing the gender binary.

B. Residential Space

Gender-inclusive housing options should be available to all students, with no requirement for special medical documentation or approval. Residential facilities must offer all-gender restrooms and showers that are private, accessible, and secure. Housing assignments should prioritize students' gender identities rather than their sex assigned at birth. These inclusive options must be priced similarly to traditional housing. Residential staff should be trained to create an affirming and supportive environment for gender-expansive residents.

> 9.B.1 Housing options include gender-inclusive living arrangements available to all students without requiring special documentation or medical approval.
> 9.B.2 Residential buildings include all-gender restrooms and shower facilities that are accessible, private, and secure.
> 9.B.3 Room assignment processes respect students' gender identities rather than sex assigned at birth.
> 9.B.4 Gender-inclusive housing options are available at comparable costs and locations to traditional housing.
> 9.B.5 Residential staff receive comprehensive training on creating affirming environments for transgender and gender-expansive residents.

C. Learning Environments

Classroom seating and arrangements should avoid reinforcing traditional gender divisions. Academic spaces, including libraries and study areas, should be designed to welcome gender diversity. Visual materials and imagery in learning environments should reflect a variety of gender expressions and identities. Lab and studio spaces must be accessible and respectful of transgender and gender-expansive students' needs. Performance spaces should provide gender-neutral preparation areas, including dressing rooms.

> 9.C.1 Classroom seating and arrangements allow students to participate without reinforcing binary gender divisions or stereotypes.
> 9.C.2 Study spaces, libraries, and academic support areas incorporate design elements that welcome gender diversity.
> 9.C.3 Learning spaces include imagery and visual elements representing diverse gender expressions and identities.
> 9.C.4 Laboratory and studio spaces have equitable access policies that respect the needs of transgender and gender-expansive students.
> 9.C.5 Performance and presentation spaces offer gender-neutral dressing rooms and preparation areas.

D. Campus Navigation & Wayfinding

Campus maps, directories, and digital navigation systems must clearly mark all-gender facilities. Signage should use inclusive symbols and language, and be designed to help users easily locate these spaces. Building entrances and accessible routes must be clearly visible and prioritize safety for transgender and gender-expansive individuals. Emergency evacuation plans must account for the specific needs of these students, particularly in gendered spaces.

> 9.D.1 Campus maps, directories, and navigation systems clearly identify gender-inclusive facilities.
> 9.D.2 Digital wayfinding, maps, directories, and mobile application tools enable users to locate the nearest all-gender facilities across campus.. Directional signage incorporates inclusive symbols and language.

9.D.3 Building entrances and accessible routes are clearly marked to enhance safety for transgender and gender-expansive individuals.

9.D.4 Emergency evacuation and crisis management plans consider the needs of transgender and gender-expansive individuals, especially in gendered facilities.

E. Symbolic & Representational Elements

Public art, monuments, and displays should acknowledge and represent gender diversity. Commemorative markers should highlight the contributions of transgender and gender-expansive individuals. Institutional branding and marketing materials must reflect diverse gender expressions.

9.E.1 Historical markers and commemorative spaces acknowledge contributions from transgender and gender-expansive individuals.

9.E.2 Institutional imagery in marketing materials, websites, and public spaces represents diverse gender expressions.

9.E.3 Display areas for student work and achievements include the contributions of transgender and gender-expansive community members.

9.E.4 Flags, banners, and other symbolic representations include transgender and non-binary pride symbols at appropriate times and locations.

F. Community & Social Spaces

Informal gathering spaces should be designed to accommodate people of all gender identities. Designated areas for transgender and gender-expansive community building should be provided. Shared spaces must incorporate elements that signal inclusivity. Lounge areas should allow for flexibility in seating and privacy to accommodate a wide range of body types and personal preferences. Student organization spaces should have policies that support gender inclusion in their usage and allocation. Informal gathering spaces are designed to be welcoming and accessible to people of all gender identities.

9.F.1 Dedicated spaces exist for transgender and gender-expansive community building and support.

9.F.2 General community spaces incorporate design elements that signal inclusion for transgender and gender-expansive individuals.

9.F.3 Lounge and relaxation areas include fixtures and furnishings that accommodate diverse body types and personal space preferences.

9.F.4 Student organization spaces have policies promoting gender inclusion in their use and allocation.

G. Health & Wellness Spaces

Health centers should include private intake areas to ensure confidentiality during registration. Medical exam rooms must be designed with transgender and gender-expansive patients' privacy needs in mind. Counseling and mental health spaces must provide confidential, affirming care for gender-expansive students. Wellness and recreation areas should include private changing options, and all-gender facilities should be available.

9.G.1 Campus health centers include private intake areas that protect confidentiality during registration and check-in.

9.G.2 Medical exam rooms are designed with attention to privacy concerns specific to transgender and gender-expansive patients.

9.G.3 Counseling and mental health facilities provide confidential, affirming environments for transgender and gender-expansive clients.

9.G.4 Wellness and recreation spaces offer private changing options and all-gender facilities.

9.G.5 Counseling/mental health and health center staff are trained in providing gender affirming patient care, support, and referrals to resources.

9.G.6 Directional signage to health and wellness services uses inclusive language and imagery.

H. Safety & Security

Emergency phones and safety systems should be placed in areas where transgender and gender-expansive individuals may be most vulnerable. Security cameras must respect privacy, particularly near restroom entrances, while ensuring appropriate coverage of surrounding areas. Lighting plans should prioritize pathways to gender-inclusive facilities. Safety assessments should be regularly conducted, focusing on the needs of transgender and gender-expansive individuals. Campus designs should promote visibility and minimize isolation.

9.H.1 Emergency phones and safety systems are located with consideration for areas where transgender and gender-expansive individuals may be vulnerable.

9.H.2 Security cameras respect privacy in transitional spaces like restroom entrances while ensuring adequate coverage of adjacent areas.

9.H.3 Campus lighting plans prioritize pathways to gender-inclusive facilities.

9.H.4 Safety assessments consider the specific needs of transgender and gender-expansive individuals.

9.H.5 Space design incorporates principles that enhance visibility and reduce isolation.

STANDARD 10
ADMINISTRATIVE AND ACADEMIC OFFICES, CENTERS, AND DEPARTMENTS

THIS STANDARD PROVIDES comprehensive guidelines for academic and student services departments, campus offices, and specialized centers (collectively referred to as "organizational units") to embed gender inclusivity into their daily operations, practices, service delivery, and community engagement. While institutional-level policies establish the foundation for gender inclusion, the lived experiences of transgender and gender-expansive community members are often most directly shaped by their interactions with individual departments, offices, and centers. These units serve as the primary touch-points for students, faculty, and staff, making their commitment to inclusive practices essential for creating authentic support and belonging.

Academic and student services departments influence student success through advising relationships, classroom environments, research opportunities, and departmental culture. Campus offices—from financial aid to career services to the counseling center to student activities—provide critical services that can either affirm or alienate gender-expansive individuals. Specialized centers and programs create focused experiences, communities, and resources that significantly impact campus climate and individual well-being.

This standard recognizes that effective gender inclusion requires intentional action at the organizational unit level, where policies become practice and institutional values become lived experiences. It provides a framework for departments, offices, and centers to assess their current practices, develop inclusive approaches, and continuously improve their capacity to serve all community members authentically and effectively.

A. Leadership and Governance

Organizational unit leadership plays a crucial role in establishing inclusive cultures through visible commitment, resource allocation, and accountability structures. Leaders must model inclusive behavior while creating systems that embed gender inclusivity into all aspects of operations. Strong leadership fosters an environment where staff feel empowered and equipped to uphold inclusive practices, and where students experience consistent, authentic support at every point of engagement with the organizational unit.

    10.A.1 Organizational unit leaders publicly articulate their commitment to gender inclusion through mission statements, communications, and resource allocation decisions that prioritize inclusive practices.

    10.A.2 Leadership teams include individuals with demonstrated expertise and commitment to supporting transgender and gender-expansive community members.

    10.A.3 Organizational unit governance structures include formal mechanisms for transgender and gender-expansive community members to provide input on policies, procedures, practices, and services.

    10.A.4 Performance evaluations for unit leaders include specific metrics related to advancing gender inclusion and creating supportive environments.

    10.A.5 Leadership development programs for organizational unit administrators include comprehensive training on gender identity, inclusive practices, and bias mitigation.

    10.A.6 Organizational unit leaders regularly communicate progress on gender inclusion initiatives to stakeholders and demonstrate ongoing commitment through concrete actions and resource investments.

B. Communication and Language Practices

All unit communications—from websites and publications to emails and signage—should consistently use gender-inclusive language and imagery that welcomes and affirms diverse gender identities while avoiding binary assumptions.

    10.B.1 Unit websites, publications, and marketing materials use gender-inclusive language consistently and feature diverse gender representation in imagery and testimonials.

10.B.2 Email signatures, directories, and staff communications normalize pronoun sharing while maintaining it as voluntary and regularly updating systems to reflect legal or chosen names and pronouns.

10.B.3 Forms and intake processes developed by the unit include gender identity options beyond the binary and allow for chosen name usage across all platforms.

10.B.4 Signage, displays, wayfinding, and visual communications avoid unnecessarily gendered language.

10.B.5 Waiting areas, meeting rooms, and common spaces display materials that signal inclusion for transgender and gender-expansive individuals, such as pride flags, inclusive imagery, or resource information.

10.B.6 Social media presence and digital communications reflect gender diversity and use inclusive hashtags, language, and imagery that welcome transgender and gender-expansive community members.

10.B.7 Organizational unit communications protocols establish clear guidelines for respectful language use and provide mechanisms for addressing misgendering or insensitive communications when they occur.

C. Service Delivery and Programming

Services, programs, and activities should be designed and delivered in ways that are accessible, affirming, and responsive to the needs of transgender and gender-expansive individuals while avoiding assumptions about gender identity or expression. By integrating inclusive language and visual representation into every touchpoint, organizational units signal their commitment to gender diversity and reduce barriers to engagement, foster trust, and create spaces where transgender and gender-expansive community members feel recognized, valued, and safe.

10.C.1 Service delivery protocols ensure that all staff use chosen names and pronouns consistently and have clear procedures for updating records when individuals provide new information.

10.C.2 Programming and events avoid unnecessary gender segregation and design activities that are inclusive of all gender identities and expressions.

10.C.3 Advising, counseling, and support services include staff with specific training and expertise in supporting transgender and gender-expansive individuals.

10.C.4 Services accommodate diverse needs related to gender identity, including flexible scheduling, private consultation options, and referrals to appropriate campus and community resources.

10.C.5 When applicable, programming includes consistent opportunities to celebrate gender diversity and educate the broader community about inclusive practices and transgender experiences.

10.C.6 Service evaluation and feedback mechanisms specifically assess how effective the unit serves transgender and gender-expansive community members and use this information for continuous service improvement.

D. Physical Environment and Accessibility

The physical and virtual spaces maintained by organizational units play a critical role in fostering safety, belonging, and affirmation for transgender and gender-expansive students. Thoughtful design, inclusive signage, and accessible facilities help ensure that all individuals feel welcome and supported, while private consultation areas provide essential spaces for confidential discussions related to gender identity and transitions. For units such as multicultural centers and International Programs offices, careful attention to the unique risks faced by students—including pressures from families, communities, and cultural contexts both domestic and abroad—is essential.

10.D.1 Organizational unit offices and spaces include clear signage directing visitors to nearby gender-neutral restrooms and other inclusive facilities.

10.D.2 Private consultation spaces are available for individuals who may need confidential support or discussion related to gender identity or transition processes.

10.D.3 Resource displays, bulletin boards, and information areas include materials relevant to transgender and gender-expansive community members and highlight supportive campus and community resources.

10.D.4 Organizational units, including multicultural centers and International Programs offices, design physical and virtual spaces with awareness of the unique risks faced by transgender and gender-expansive students.

10.D.5 Organizational units proactively consider potential safety concerns related to family, cultural, and community pressures—both domestic and international—

and implement strategies to protect privacy, provide confidential support, and reduce exposure to harm.

E. Staff Training and Development

Ongoing staff training is essential for creating a campus environment where transgender and gender-expansive students feel supported, affirmed, and safe. All organizational unit staff should develop both the knowledge and practical skills necessary to implement inclusive practices in their daily interactions, programming, and service delivery. Training encompasses foundational understanding of gender diversity, role-specific competencies, strategies for addressing challenging situations, and awareness of unique risks faced by students in multicultural and international contexts. Embedding gender-inclusive competencies into performance assessments and professional development plans reinforces accountability, encourages continuous growth, and strengthens the unit's capacity to serve all students equitably.

10.E.1 New staff orientation includes mandatory training on gender identity, inclusive language, and unit-specific protocols for supporting transgender and gender-expansive individuals.

10.E.2 Annual professional development requirements include content on evolving best practices in gender inclusion and updates on legal, policy, and cultural changes affecting transgender communities.

10.E.3 Staff receive specialized training relevant to their roles, such as advisors learning about name change processes, career counselors understanding workplace transition issues, or program coordinators designing inclusive activities.

10.E.4 Training programs include opportunities for staff to examine their own biases, intercultural competency, inclusive communication practices, and develop skills for addressing challenging situations with sensitivity.

10.E.5 Staff receive specialized training to recognize and address the heightened risks faced by transgender and gender-expansive students in multicultural center and international program contexts.

10.E.6 Organizational units maintain relationships with campus and community experts who can provide ongoing consultation, training, and support for staff development in gender inclusion.

10.E.7 Staff competency in gender-inclusive practices is included in performance assessment and professional development planning processes.

F. Community Building and Outreach

Organizational units play a vital role in cultivating inclusive, supportive, and connected communities for transgender and gender-expansive students. Institutions should be intentional about programming, targeted outreach, and strategic partnerships in order to create spaces and opportunities that foster belonging, build allyship, and amplify diverse voices across campus and beyond. Inclusive mentoring programs, peer support initiatives, and collaborative events not only provide direct support to transgender and gender-expansive participants but also educate the broader campus community, raising awareness of gender diversity and advancing a vibrant campus experience.

10.F.1 Unit programming includes regular community-building activities that bring together individuals across gender identities while creating specific opportunities for transgender and gender-expansive community members to connect.

10.F.2 Outreach efforts specifically target transgender and gender-expansive populations through appropriate channels, partnerships, and messaging that demonstrates understanding and support.

10.F.3 Organizational units collaborate regularly with LGBTQIA+ organizations, transgender advocacy groups, and other relevant campus and community partners to strengthen support networks.

10.F.4 Mentoring programs, peer support initiatives, and community engagement opportunities are designed to be inclusive and provide specific support for transgender and gender-expansive participants.

10.F.5 Organizational unit actively promotes broader campus education about gender diversity through speakers, workshops, resource sharing, and collaborative programming with other departments and centers.

10.F.6 Alum and community engagement efforts include and celebrate transgender and gender-expansive former students and community members while maintaining appropriate privacy and consent protocols.

G. Resource Allocation and Support

Strategic allocation of resources is essential for ensuring that organizational units can effectively support transgender and gender-expansive students while sustaining inclusive practices over time. Budgeting, staff time, technology, and programming must all be intentionally directed to initiatives that promote gender inclusivity, including training, emergency support, and specialized services. Technology and information systems should facilitate accurate use of chosen names, pronouns, and gender identities while safeguarding privacy, and units should maintain up-to-date knowledge of campus and community resources to connect students with appropriate support.

- 10.G.1 Budget planning includes dedicated funding lines for gender inclusion initiatives, staff training, programming, and resource development.
- 10.G.2 Emergency support funds or mechanisms are available to address acute needs that may disproportionately affect transgender and gender-expansive individuals.
- 10.G.3 Technology systems and platforms used by the unit accommodate chosen names, pronouns, and gender identities with appropriate privacy protections and easy updating processes.
- 10.G.4 Unit maintains current information about campus and community resources relevant to transgender and gender-expansive individuals and provides referrals and connections as appropriate.
- 10.G.5 Staff time and expertise are allocated to ensure adequate support for gender inclusion initiatives while preventing burnout among staff members who are themselves from marginalized communities.

H. Assessment and Continuous Improvement

Ongoing assessment and evaluation are essential for organizational units to ensure that transgender and gender-expansive students receive equitable, affirming, and effective support. By systematically gathering feedback through surveys, program evaluations, and direct input from community members, units can identify strengths, gaps, and areas for growth in policies, practices, and services. Tracking quantitative and qualitative metrics—from satisfaction and utilization rates to student progression and outcomes—enables data-informed decision-making and accountability. Incorporating this feedback into program development, policy changes, and professional development ensures continuous improvement and effectiveness.

> 10.H.1 Regular assessment tools measure the experiences and satisfaction of transgender and gender-expansive individuals who interact with the unit, with appropriate privacy protections and voluntary participation.
>
> 10.H.2 Organizational unit and campus climate surveys and feedback mechanisms specifically address issues of inclusion, respect, and support for diverse gender identities while disaggregating data when appropriate.
>
> 10.H.3 Annual program reviews include specific evaluation of gender inclusion efforts, including tracking of student performance from entry, progression, to completion, with recommendations for improvement and accountability for implementing changes.
>
> 10.H.4 Organizational units track relevant metrics such as utilization rates, satisfaction scores, and outcome measures for transgender and gender-expansive participants in unit programs and services.
>
> 10.H.5 Feedback from transgender and gender-expansive community members directly informs program development, policy revision, and service improvement initiatives within the unit.
>
> 10.H.6 Best practices and successful innovations are documented and shared with other units and institutions to contribute to broader advancement of gender inclusion in higher education.

I. Crisis Response and Support

Organizational units must be prepared to respond swiftly and effectively to crises affecting transgender and gender-expansive community members, recognizing that these students may face unique vulnerabilities during emergencies or challenging situations. Crisis protocols should integrate inclusive practices, prioritize safety, and ensure access to knowledgeable resources and specialized support. Staff training equips personnel to recognize signs of distress related to gender identity, provide appropriate interventions, and make timely referrals while maintaining confidentiality and respect for privacy. Communication during crises must be deliberate, using inclusive language and addressing the specific safety and informational needs of transgender and gender-expansive students.

10.I.1 Crisis response protocols include specific considerations for supporting transgender and gender-expansive individuals who may face unique vulnerabilities or challenges during emergencies or difficult situations.

10.I.2 Staff are trained to recognize signs of distress that may be related to gender identity issues and know how to provide appropriate support and referrals to specialized resources.

10.I.3 Unit maintains current information about campus and community crisis resources that are knowledgeable about and supportive of transgender and gender-expansive individuals.

10.I.4 Communication during crises uses inclusive language and considers the specific information needs and safety concerns of transgender and gender-expansive community members.

10.I.5 Post-incident recovery, crisis support and follow-up services are designed to address ongoing needs while respecting privacy and individual preferences for continued engagement with the unit.

STANDARD 11
HEALTH AND WELLNESS SERVICES

TO FULLY SUPPORT transgender and gender-expansive students, institutions must ensure that health and wellness services are intentionally inclusive, accessible, and responsive to their unique needs. These services should provide healthcare that affirms students' gender identities and protects their privacy at every step of care. Institutions should actively remove barriers to access by addressing financial, logistical, and physical obstacles, while also recognizing the complex social, economic, and health-related challenges that students with diverse gender identities may face. Health and wellness programs should integrate mental health support, medical care, and health education in a way that promotes holistic well-being. By embedding these standards into policies, training, and everyday practices, campuses create environments where transgender and gender-expansive students feel respected, safe, and empowered to thrive academically, socially, and personally.

A. Medical Services

Campus clinics, campus owned and contracted, should establish comprehensive gender-affirming care programs that integrate hormone therapy within established frameworks like WPATH guidelines, while ensuring that all administrative systems and documentation honor students' chosen names, pronouns, and self-identified gender in ways that respect anatomical diversity. These efforts must be supported by insurance plans that provide full coverage for transition-related services, alongside well-trained clinicians who can deliver affirming care directly and maintain strong referral partnerships to address specialized needs that extend beyond campus resources.

> 11.A.1 Campus health centers offer gender-affirming healthcare including hormone therapy initiation and monitoring, following current WPATH Standards of Care.
>
> 11.A.2 Medical intake forms use inclusive language, allow for self-identified gender identity, chosen name and pronouns, and recognize anatomical diversity.
>
> 11.A.3 Campus health insurance policies explicitly cover gender-affirming care including hormones, surgeries, and related services without exclusions.
>
> 11.A.4 Medical staff receive comprehensive and ongoing training in gender-affirming healthcare, including training on supporting transgender and gender-expansive patients.
>
> 11.A.5 Health centers maintain referral relationships with gender-affirming specialists for services not available on campus.

B. Mental Health Support

Counseling teams must include professionals with expertise in supporting transgender and non-binary individuals. Care should follow an informed consent model, not gatekeeping. Therapists must be qualified to write transition-related documentation and offer identity-affirming group spaces. Crisis protocols should reflect an understanding of gender-specific risks and needs.

> 11.B.1 Counseling services include providers specifically trained in supporting transgender and gender-expansive individuals through various aspects of identity development and transition.
>
> 11.B.2 Mental health professionals follow an informed consent model rather than gatekeeping when supporting gender-expansive clients.
>
> 11.B.3 Therapists are qualified to write support letters for gender-affirming medical care when requested by clients, following current professional guidelines.
>
> 11.B.4 Group therapy and support options include specific groups for transgender and gender-expansive students.
>
> 11.B.5 Crisis response protocols include specific considerations for supporting transgender and gender-expansive students in crisis.

C. Accessible Care

Services must be financially and logistically reachable—through sliding scale fees, free care options, telehealth, and extended hours. Same-day appointments should be available for urgent needs. Physical spaces must be ADA-compliant, with attention to students whose gender identity intersects with disability.

- 11.C.1 Sliding scale fees, subsidized services, or free options exist for transgender and gender-expansive students who may face financial barriers to care.
- 11.C.2 Telehealth options are available for students who may not feel comfortable accessing in-person services.
- 11.C.3 Extended or flexible appointment hours accommodate students with complex schedules due to work, academic, or other commitments.
- 11.C.4 Walk-in or same-day appointment options exist for urgent gender-affirming care needs.
- 11.C.5 Services are physically accessible to students with disabilities, with specific attention to the intersection of disability and gender identity.

D. Confidentiality and Privacy

Sensitive information—such as gender identity and transition history—must be kept strictly private. Systems should use affirmed names and pronouns across interfaces, with safeguards against misgendering or inadvertent disclosure. Staff must be trained in nuanced privacy concerns, including when legal names are required.

- 11.D.1 Health and counseling records maintain strict confidentiality about gender identity, transition status, and birth-assigned sex.
- 11.D.2 Electronic health records systems correctly display chosen names and pronouns while maintaining necessary medical history.
- 11.D.3 Waiting areas and check-in processes are designed to protect privacy and prevent inadvertent disclosure of gender identity.
- 11.D.4 Clear confidentiality protocols exist for communication between health services and other campus departments.
- 11.D.5 Staff are trained on specific privacy considerations related to gender identity, including legal name usage requirements and exceptions.

E. Health Education and Outreach

Public health messaging should reflect diverse identities and use inclusive, non-binary language. Programming must cover topics relevant to transgender students—sexual wellness, mental health, substance use—and be developed in collaboration with LGBTQIA+ resources and organizations.

> 11.E.1 Health promotion materials represent diverse gender identities and use inclusive language when discussing bodies and health issues.
>
> 11.E.2 Educational workshops and resources specifically address health topics relevant to transgender and gender-expansive individuals.
>
> 11.E.3 Sexual health education includes information relevant to people of all gender identities and expressions.
>
> 11.E.4 Self-harm and suicide prevention and intervention programs address the specific risk factors affecting transgender and gender-expansive communities.
>
> 11.E.5 Substance use prevention and intervention programs address the specific risk factors affecting transgender and gender-expansive communities.
>
> 11.E.6 Health and wellness programming regularly collaborates with LGBTQIA+ resource centers and student organizations.

F. Staff Competency and Representation

All staff—from front desk to clinical providers—must be trained in gender-inclusive communication and care. Providers need specialized knowledge relevant to their disciplines, with opportunities for continuous learning. Hiring practices should value lived experience and demonstrated commitment to trans-inclusive healthcare.

> 11.F.1 All health and wellness staff, including front desk and support personnel, receive training on gender-inclusive practices and terminology.
>
> 11.F.2 Medical and mental health providers receive specialized training in gender-affirming care relevant to their roles.
>
> 11.F.3 Health and wellness services employ staff members with lived experience and/or significant professional expertise in transgender healthcare.
>
> 11.F.4 Regular professional development opportunities keep staff current on evolving best practices in gender-affirming care.

GENDER INCLUSIVITY STANDARDS AND EXPECTATIONS IN HIGHER EDUCATION   75

11.F.5 Staff evaluation includes metrics related to competency in serving transgender and gender-expansive patients/clients.

G. Integrated Support Networks

Health and wellness teams should coordinate with LGBTQIA+ centers, academic support, housing, and external providers to ensure comprehensive care. Formal referral pathways and shared practices foster continuity. Active participation in campus inclusion efforts strengthens institutional alignment.

11.G.1 Health and wellness services maintain formal partnerships with campus LGBTQIA+ resource centers.
11.G.2 Clear referral pathways exist between counseling services, health services, and community resources for comprehensive care.
11.G.3 Health and wellness providers collaborate with residence life, academic affairs, and other campus offices to coordinate support for transitioning students.
11.G.4 Memoranda of understanding with local hospitals and specialists should be developed and assessed to ensure continuity of care for gender-affirming services.
11.G.5 Health and wellness services participate in campus-wide committees addressing transgender inclusion.

H. Assessment and Quality Improvement

Regular feedback from gender-expansive students must inform service improvements. Utilization data, satisfaction surveys, and outcome measures should be disaggregated to identify inequities. Annual reviews must assess environments, staff preparedness, and adherence to inclusive care standards.

11.H.1 Regular assessment of services includes specific measures of transgender and gender-expansive patients' experiences and outcomes.
11.H.2 Patient/client feedback mechanisms include specific questions about gender-affirming care.
11.H.3 Health and wellness services regularly review and update protocols based on current research and best practices in transgender healthcare.

11.H.4 Services track utilization rates among transgender and gender-expansive students to identify potential barriers to access.

11.H.5 Annual service reviews include evaluating the physical environment, protocols, and staff competencies related to gender-affirming care.

STANDARD 12
DATA COLLECTION AND ASSESSMENT

HIGHER EDUCATION INSTITUTIONS play a critical role in fostering equity and inclusion when they intentionally embed gender-expansive practices throughout all aspects of data collection, assessment, and accountability. By centering the lived experiences of transgender and gender-expansive students and employees, institutions can ensure that their processes are affirming, informed, and ethically sound. Thoughtfully designed data collection tools allow individuals to self-identify in ways that reflect their authentic identities, while robust privacy protections safeguard sensitive information. Assessment practices that combine quantitative and qualitative methods capture nuanced experiences, and longitudinal tracking enables institutions to monitor progress over time. Beyond data collection, careful analysis, reporting, and the strategic use of findings translate insights into actionable improvements in policy, programming, and campus climate. Transparency, ethical research practices, and continuous professional development ensure that these efforts are both accountable and responsive to the evolving needs of gender-expansive communities. Ultimately, these standards guide institutions to cultivate environments where all members feel recognized, respected, and supported through evidence-based decision-making and ongoing institutional learning.

A. Identity Data Collection

Institutions must design demographic tools that reflect the diversity of gender identities beyond the binary. Categories should be co-developed with transgender and gender-expansive communities, using current and respectful terminology. Distinctions between gender identity and sex assigned at birth must be clearly explained, with the option to decline responses without restricting access to services. Consistency across all institutional surveys enables meaningful comparison and longitudinal tracking.

> 12.A.1 Demographic forms include gender identity options beyond the binary, with categories developed in consultation with transgender and gender-expansive community members.
>
> 12.A.2 Gender identity questions are distinct from sex assigned at birth questions, with clear explanations for why each type of information is being collected.
>
> 12.A.3 Systems allow individuals to decline to state their gender identity without preventing form completion or access to services.
>
> 12.A.4 Data collection tools use current, culturally responsive terminology for gender identity categories that are regularly reviewed and updated.
>
> 12.A.5 All institutional surveys include consistent gender identity questions to enable cross-survey comparisons and longitudinal tracking.

B. Privacy Protection

Robust privacy standards are essential. Access to gender identity data must be clearly defined and limited, with justifications documented. Systems must protect historical information and separate legal identifiers from chosen names and identities. Transparent data usage statements and specific breach protocols ensure trust and safety for individuals disclosing sensitive information.

> 12.B.1 Clear policies govern who has access to gender identity data and under what circumstances.
>
> 12.B.2 Data systems protect historical name and gender information, with strictly limited access and clear justification requirements.
>
> 12.B.3 Data collection notifications explain how gender identity information will be used, stored, and protected.
>
> 12.B.4 Data storage systems maintain appropriate separation between chosen names/gender identities and legal names/sex markers.
>
> 12.B.5 Data breach protocols include specific consideration of potential harms related to disclosure of gender identity and specific people information.

C. Assessment Design

Effective assessment practices should incorporate comprehensive climate measures that specifically capture the experiences of transgender and gender-expansive community members through a thoughtful blend of quantitative and qualitative methodologies that together provide both breadth and nuanced depth. These assessment instruments must undergo careful review by gender-expansive stakeholders to ensure they avoid reinforcing binary assumptions in both their questioning and analytical frameworks, while establishing robust long-term tracking systems that enable institutions to monitor campus climate changes and maintain responsiveness to the evolving needs of these communities.

12.C.1 Qualitative data collection methods supplement quantitative methods to capture nuanced experiences related to gender identity.

12.C.2 Assessment instruments are reviewed by transgender and gender-expansive stakeholders before implementation.

12.C.3 Data collection tools avoid unnecessary gender binaries in question wording, response options, and analysis frameworks.

12.C.4 Longitudinal assessment plans track changes in campus climate for transgender and gender-expansive individuals over time.

D. Data Analysis and Reporting

Gender identity data should be disaggregated responsibly, maintaining confidentiality—especially in small populations. Reporting avoids revealing identities, while research offices build the capacity to interpret gender data with care. Visualizations must affirm diversity without reinforcing binary frameworks, and intersectional analyses are pursued when viable. Analysis practices include disaggregation by gender identity while maintaining appropriate sample sizes to protect individual privacy.

12.D.1 Reports using gender identity data avoid practices that might inadvertently reveal individual identities in small populations.

12.D.2 Institutional research offices develop expertise in appropriate methods for analyzing gender identity data.

12.D.3 Data visualization follows best practices for representing gender diversity without reinforcing binary frameworks.

12.D.4 Intersectional analyses examine how gender identity interacts with other identity factors, when sample sizes permit.

E. Data Usage and Impact

Assessment findings must translate into action. Gender-related data informs strategic planning, resource allocation, and policy development. Regular sharing with campus leadership supports transparency, while benchmarks and KPIs track progress. Results are linked to accountability structures, ensuring ongoing commitment to inclusion.

12.E.1 Assessment results directly inform strategic planning, resource allocation, and policy development related to gender inclusion.

12.E.2 Data on transgender and gender-expansive experiences is regularly shared with relevant campus committees and leadership groups.

12.E.3 Assessment findings are used to establish benchmarks and measurable goals for improving gender inclusion.

12.E.4 Regular reporting cycles track progress on key performance indicators related to transgender and gender-expansive student success.

12.E.5 Assessment results are connected to accountability measures for departments and units across the institution.

F. Transparency and Communication

Institutions must communicate clearly about why data is collected and how it will be used. Reports are shared with privacy protections in place and include concrete action steps. Assessment outcomes are contextualized within broader DEI efforts, with transgender and gender-expansive communities actively engaged in interpretation and messaging.

12.F.1 Communication about assessment findings includes specific action steps based on the data.

12.F.2 Data collection purposes and outcomes are clearly communicated to potential participants.

12.F.3 Assessment findings related to gender inclusion are contextualized within broader institutional diversity, equity, and inclusion efforts.

GENDER INCLUSIVITY STANDARDS AND EXPECTATIONS IN HIGHER EDUCATION   81

12.F.4 Transgender and gender-expansive community members are consulted in the interpretation and communication of relevant assessment findings.

12.F.5 Summary reports of gender inclusion assessment data are made available to the campus community with appropriate privacy protections.

G. Research Ethics

Research involving gender-expansive individuals must be grounded in ethics and community accountability. IRBs are trained in gender-specific considerations, and research protocols prioritize protection from harm and misrepresentation. Participatory approaches are encouraged, and findings must benefit the communities involved while protecting privacy.

12.G.1 Institutional Review Boards receive training on ethics considerations specific to research involving transgender and gender-expansive populations.

12.G.2 Research protocols involving transgender and gender-expansive participants include appropriate safeguards against exploitation and misrepresentation.

12.G.3 Campus research on transgender issues follows community-based participatory research principles when appropriate.

12.G.4 Publication of research findings maintains appropriate privacy protections for transgender and gender-expansive participants.

12.G.5 Research benefits are shared with transgender and gender-expansive communities who participated in or are affected by the research.

H. Continuous Improvement

Gender inclusion practices are never static. Institutions are expected to regularly review and refine assessment tools and strategies. Committees must include gender identity expertise, and staff should receive ongoing training. Inclusion metrics are built into institutional effectiveness plans, with emerging best practices from peer institutions guiding further evolution.

12.H.1 Assessment instruments and methods are regularly reviewed and updated to reflect evolving understanding of gender identity.

12.H.2 Data governance committees include expertise related to gender identity data collection and usage.

12.H.3 Assessment professionals receive ongoing professional development related to inclusive data collection and analysis practices.

12.H.4 Institutional effectiveness measures include specific metrics related to gender inclusion progress.

12.H.5 High-impact practices from peer institutions inform ongoing refinement of gender inclusion assessment methods.

STANDARD 13
EXECUTIVE SEARCH FIRMS

THIS STANDARD ESTABLISHES comprehensive guidelines for executive search firms to ensure equitable, respectful, and supportive recruitment processes for gender-expansive candidates while educating client institutions on inclusive practices. Search firms play a critical intermediary role in executive recruitment and must demonstrate measurable competency in gender-inclusive practices, from initial candidate identification through final placement and beyond. These standards recognize that executive search firms significantly influence both candidate experience and institutional hiring decisions, requiring specialized training, systematic processes, and ongoing accountability to create truly inclusive executive recruitment pipelines.

A. Firm Capacity and Training

Executive search firms should develop internal expertise and systematic approaches to gender-inclusive recruitment that permeate all aspects of their operations and staff competencies.

> 13.A.1 Firm leadership demonstrates measurable commitment to gender-inclusive practices through public diversity statements, resource allocation, and partnership with gender-expansive professional organizations.
>
> 13.A.2 All search consultants and support staff receive comprehensive training on

gender identity, expression, and inclusion, with annual updates on evolving best practices and legal requirements.

13.A.3 Search firms maintain documented policies and procedures specifically addressing gender-inclusive recruitment practices, candidate support protocols, and bias mitigation strategies.

13.A.4 Internal firm systems (databases, communication platforms, reporting tools) accommodate chosen names, pronouns, and gender identities with robust privacy protections and easy updating capabilities.

B. Candidate Sourcing and Outreach

Search firms should actively and systematically identify and engage gender-expansive candidates through targeted outreach and inclusive sourcing strategies.

13.B.1 Candidate sourcing strategies explicitly include gender-expansive professional networks, associations, and specialized job boards to ensure diverse candidate pools.

13.B.2 Initial outreach communications use gender-inclusive language and clearly articulate the firm's commitment to supporting gender-expansive candidates throughout the search process.

13.B.3 Search firms maintain ongoing relationships with gender-expansive executive talent through regular networking, mentorship programs, and professional development opportunities.

13.B.4 Candidate databases and tracking systems disaggregate data by gender identity to monitor and improve recruitment effectiveness for gender-expansive executives.

C. Search Process Management

Search firms should implement systematic processes that eliminate bias and create inclusive experiences for all candidates while supporting client institutions in inclusive decision-making.

13.C.1 Search committee training includes comprehensive education on gender identity, unconscious bias mitigation, and inclusive interviewing practices before candidate evaluation begins.

13.C.2 Candidate evaluation criteria and processes are reviewed and refined to eliminate gender bias, with particular attention to leadership assessments that may disadvantage gender-expansive candidates.

13.C.3 Interview scheduling, venue selection, and logistics accommodate candidate needs related to gender identity and expression, including accessible restroom access and respectful environment considerations.

13.C.4 Reference checking processes include specific training for search consultants on asking appropriate questions and avoiding bias when discussing gender-expansive candidates with former colleagues.

D. Candidate Support and Advocacy

Search firms should provide comprehensive support to gender-expansive candidates throughout the recruitment process, serving as advocates and resources for successful participation.

13.D.1 Dedicated candidate support protocols address the unique needs of gender-expansive executives, including preparation for potential bias, institutional culture assessment, and negotiation support.

13.D.2 Search consultants receive specialized training on supporting gender-expansive candidates through interview preparation, addressing potential concerns, and providing emotional and strategic support.

13.D.3 Confidential resources exist for gender-expansive candidates to address concerns or challenges during the search process without jeopardizing their candidacy.

13.D.4 Search firms provide detailed information about institutional climate, policies, and support systems relevant to gender-expansive employees to enable informed candidate decision-making.

E. Client Education and Consultation

Search firms should actively educate client institutions on inclusive hiring practices and serve as consultants on creating welcoming environments for gender-expansive executive candidates.

> 13.E.1 Client consultation includes assessment of institutional readiness to support gender-expansive executives, with recommendations for policy and culture improvements before search launch.
> 13.E.2 Search firms provide ongoing education to client institutions about legal requirements, best practices, and benefits of gender-inclusive executive recruitment.
> 13.E.3 Contract negotiations with client institutions include explicit commitments to inclusive search processes and non-discrimination protections for all candidates.
> 13.E.4 Search firms decline to work with client institutions that refuse to implement basic gender-inclusive practices or that demonstrate clear bias against gender-expansive candidates.

F. Accountability and Continuous Improvement

Search firms should implement systematic accountability measures and commit to ongoing improvement in gender-inclusive practices through data collection, assessment, and refinement.

> 13.F.1 Regular assessment of search outcomes includes analysis of gender-expansive candidate progression through search processes and placement success rates.
> 13.F.2 Client and candidate feedback systems specifically measure experiences related to gender inclusion, with results used for continuous process improvement.
> 13.F.3 Search firms publicly report annual data on gender-inclusive recruitment efforts, outcomes, and improvement initiatives to demonstrate accountability and progress.
> 13.F.4 Ongoing partnerships with gender-expansive professional organizations and advocacy groups provide external feedback and guidance for improving search firm practices.

G. Post-Placement Support

Search firms should provide continued support to ensure the successful integration and retention of gender-expansive executives in their new institutional roles.

13.G.1 Transition support includes follow-up consultation with both candidates and institutions during the first year of placement to address any inclusion-related challenges.

13.G.2 Search firms maintain relationships with placed executives to provide ongoing career support, mentorship connections, and professional development opportunities.

13.G.3 Institutional consultation continues post-placement to support client organizations in creating inclusive environments that enable gender-expansive executives to thrive and advance.

CHAPTER 14
TOWARD A FUTURE OF BELONGING AND EXCELLENCE

THE TEN STANDARDS presented in this volume represent more than a comprehensive guide to gender-inclusive practices in higher education—they constitute a blueprint for institutional transformation that can fundamentally reshape how colleges and universities fulfill their mission of fostering human flourishing and advancing knowledge. From the initial moment of admissions contact through the ongoing relationships maintained with alumni, from classroom pedagogy to campus infrastructure, from employee recruitment to executive leadership, these standards provide a roadmap for creating environments where all community members can thrive authentically and contribute fully to the educational enterprise.

Yet as we reach the conclusion of this framework, it is essential to emphasize what these standards are not. They are not a checklist to be completed, boxes to be checked, or compliance requirements to be minimally satisfied. Rather, they represent an integrated approach to cultural transformation that requires sustained commitment, ongoing learning, and genuine partnership with the communities they seek to serve. The true measure of success will not be found in the number of policies revised or training sessions completed, but in the lived experiences of transgender and gender-expansive students, faculty, and staff who encounter these institutions as places of genuine welcome, affirmation, and opportunity.

The interconnected nature of these standards reflects a fundamental understanding: gender inclusion cannot be achieved through isolated initiatives or superficial modifications to existing systems. When admissions processes honor diverse gender identities, they set expectations for campus climate that must be fulfilled through inclusive pedagogy, supportive student life programming, comprehensive health services, and affirming physical spaces. When institutions recruit and retain gender-expansive employees, they create role models and advocates who enhance the experience for students while contributing essential perspectives to institutional governance and decision-making. When data collection practices capture the full spectrum of gender diversity, they enable evidence-based improvements that benefit all community members.

The Ripple Effects of Inclusion

The benefits of implementing these standards extend far beyond their impact on transgender and gender-expansive individuals, though their primary purpose is to ensure that these community members can flourish authentically. When institutions create truly inclusive environments, they enhance educational excellence for everyone. Students learn to navigate diversity and complexity, skills essential for success in an increasingly interconnected world. Faculty and staff develop greater cultural competency and inclusive pedagogical practices that benefit all learners. Institutional cultures become more innovative, adaptive, and responsive to changing needs and circumstances.

Moreover, gender-inclusive practices often reveal and address broader systems of exclusion that may disadvantage other marginalized communities. The universal design principles that create accessible systems for gender-expansive individuals frequently enhance usability for people with disabilities, international students, first-generation college students, and others who may not fit traditional institutional assumptions. The intersectional framework that recognizes multiple identity dimensions strengthens efforts to advance racial equity, economic justice, and other dimensions of inclusion.

Leadership for Transformative Change

The implementation of these standards requires courageous leadership at every level of institutional operation. Presidents and senior administrators must allocate resources, champion policy changes, and model inclusive behavior while holding themselves and others accountable for progress. Faculty must examine their pedagogical practices, curriculum content, and assessment methods to ensure they create learning environments where all students can succeed. Student affairs professionals must design programs and services that affirm diverse identities while building bridges across different communities. Facilities managers must rethink space design and signage to create welcoming physical environments. Every community member has a role to play in creating cultures of belonging and respect.

This leadership requires both moral courage and practical competence. It demands the willingness to acknowledge past exclusions and commit to different approaches moving forward. It requires investment in professional development, community engagement, and organizational change processes that may be challenging and sometimes uncomfortable. Most importantly, it requires sustained commitment that persists through changes in leadership, budget constraints, and external pressures.

An Ongoing Journey

Perhaps most importantly, these standards recognize that creating gender-inclusive institutions is not a destination to be reached but an ongoing journey of learning, growth, and adaptation. As understanding of gender diversity continues to evolve, as new research emerges, and as institutional communities change, these practices must be continuously refined and renewed. The specific strategies that constitute best practice today may be enhanced or replaced by more effective approaches tomorrow. What remains constant is the commitment to honoring the dignity and humanity of all community members while creating conditions for their authentic participation and success.

This adaptive approach requires institutions to develop capacity for continuous improvement, including regular assessment, community feedback, and willingness to acknowledge mistakes and make corrections. It demands humility about current limitations while maintaining hope and determination for future possibilities. It recognizes that the work of inclusion is never complete but always worthy of sustained effort and investment.

A Call to Action

The standards presented in this volume represent both an invitation and a challenge to higher education institutions across the nation. They invite participation in a transformative movement that can enhance educational excellence while advancing social justice. They challenge institutions to examine fundamental assumptions, revise entrenched practices, and commit resources to creating more inclusive communities.

The urgency of this work cannot be overstated. Every day that institutions delay implementing gender-inclusive practices is another day that transgender and gender-expansive community members face unnecessary barriers, discrimination, and exclusion. Every semester that passes without inclusive curricula is a missed opportunity to prepare all students for success in diverse societies. Every year without comprehensive change represents a failure to fulfill higher education's highest aspirations for human flourishing and social progress.

Yet the opportunity is equally profound. Institutions that embrace these standards have the chance to become models of inclusion and excellence, attracting diverse talent, enhancing educational outcomes, and contributing to the creation of a more just society. They can position themselves as leaders in preparing graduates who possess not only disciplinary expertise but also the cultural competency and inclusive mindset necessary for success in an interconnected world.

The path forward requires courage, commitment, and collective action. It demands that institutional leaders embrace their moral responsibility while recognizing the profound benefits that gender inclusivity brings to educational mission and community life. Most importantly, it requires recognition that creating gender-inclusive institutions is not additional work layered onto existing responsibilities, but rather an essential dimension of educational excellence that enhances every aspect of institutional operation.

The transgender and gender-expansive students, faculty, and staff in our communities deserve nothing less than environments where they can thrive authentically and contribute fully to the collective pursuit of knowledge and understanding that defines higher education at its best. These standards provide the framework for creating such environments. The question that remains is whether institutions will embrace this opportunity for transformative change and the profound possibilities it represents for the future of higher education.

REFERENCES

American Psychological Association. (2015). *Guidelines for psychological practice with transgender and gender nonconforming people. American Psychologist, 70*(9), 832-864. https://doi.org/13.1037/a0039906.

Best Colleges. (2025, May 28). *Diversity in higher education: Facts and statistics.* https://www.bestcolleges.com/research/diversity-in-higher-education-facts-statistics/.

Butler, J. (1990). *Gender trouble: Feminism and the subversion of identity.* New York: Routledge.

Case, K. A., Kanenberg, H., Erich, S., & Tittsworth, J. (2012). Transgender inclusion in university nondiscrimination statements: Challenging gender-conforming privilege through student activism. *Journal of Social Issues, 68*(1), 145-161.

Crenshaw, K. (1989). Demarginalizing the intersection of race and sex: A Black feminist critique of antidiscrimination doctrine, feminist theory and antiracist politics. *University of Chicago Legal Forum, 1989*(1), 139-167.

Crenshaw, K. (1991). Mapping the margins: Intersectionality, identity politics, and violence against women of color. *Stanford Law Review, 43*(6), 1241-1299. https://doi.org/13.2307/1229039

Freire, P. (1970/2017). *Pedagogy of the oppressed.* Penguin Classics. (Original work published 1970).

Goldberg, A. E., & Kuvalanka, K. A. (2018). Navigating identity development and community belonging when "there are only two boxes to check": An exploratory study of nonbinary trans college students. *Journal of LGBT Youth, 15*(2), 106-131.

Goldberg, A. E., Kuvalanka, K., & Black, K. (2019). Trans students who leave college: An exploratory study of their experiences of gender minority stress. *Journal of College Student Development, 60*(4), 381-400. https://doi.org/13.1353/csd.2019.0035.

James, S. E., Herman, J. L., Rankin, S., Keisling, M., Mottet, L., & Anafi, M. (2016). *The report of the 2015 U.S. Transgender Survey.* National Center for Transgender Equality. https://transequality.org/sites/default/files/docs/usts/USTS-Full-Report-Dec17.pdf.

Kosciw, J. G., Clark, C. M., Truong, N. L., & Zongrone, A. D. (2022). *The 2021 National School Climate Survey: The experiences of LGBTQ+ youth in our nation's schools.* GLSEN. https://www.glsen.org/sites/default/files/2022-10/NSCS-2021-Full-Report.pdf.

Marine, S. B. (2011). *Stonewall's legacy: Bisexual, gay, lesbian and transgender students in higher education* (ASHE Higher Education Report, Vol. 37, No. 4). Jossey-Bass.

Top Universities. (2024, May 14). *QS Stars*. https://www.topuniversities.com/qs-stars/qs-stars/rating-universities-diversity-equity-inclusion-qs-stars.

University of California San Francisco. (2016). *Guidelines for the primary and gender-affirming care of transgender and gender nonbinary people*. UCSF Transgender Care. https://transcare.ucsf.edu/guidelines/terminology.

Times Higher Education. (2025, June 17). *University Impact Rankings for UN SDG 5: gender equality*. https://www.timeshighereducation.com/impactrankings/gender-equality.

Claude Sonnet 4, from Anthropic, was used in this manuscript between July and September of 2025 for idea generation and feedback. Drafts of standards were submitted to Claude, which then provided suggestions in terms of content, organization, and the addition of individual standards. All suggestions from Claude were edited substantially prior to publication.

ABOUT THE AUTHORS

Julia G. MaKinster (she/her), Ph.D. is a Professor of Educational Studies at Hobart and William Smith College. She is a former Vice Provost for Institutional Effectiveness and Senior Associate Provost for Curriculum, Assessment and Strategic Planning. A transwoman and queer activist, Julia's mission is to foster gender equity and inclusion in ways that improve the lives of individuals and simultaneously work to dismantle structural and institutional barriers to equity and access. With 5 books, 28 journal articles, and 6 book chapters, she focuses on educational leadership, diversity and inclusion, and issues of gender and gender identity in higher education. She regularly facilitates workshops, presentations, and multi-day institutes on gender inclusivity, academic leadership, and antiracist teaching.

Luca Lewis (he/him), Ph.D. Dr. Luca Lewis brings over 20 years of exemplary leadership and innovation experience, spanning various educational institutions. Serving currently as the Vice President of Student Affairs at Ventura College in Ventura, California, Luca is well known for advancing partnerships and maximizing institutional strengths for diverse learners and earners. Luca was a contributing author to the highly acclaimed book, *Higher Education Administration for Social Justice and Equity: Critical Perspectives for Leadership*, by Dr. Adrianna Kezar and Dr. Julie Posselt. Likewise, as a sought-after national expert, Luca carries a distinguished leadership reputation in helping institutions achieve excellence through culturally responsive teaching and learning practices, program growth and development, equity-minded leadership and decision-making, and institutional advancement. He has demonstrated experience and expertise in strengthening institutional and district-wide outcomes for communities with intersecting identities and eliminating barriers to access and success for all students.

INDEX

A
Accessibility
- ADA compliance, 55, 56, 73
- Campus facilities, 32-33, 46, 51-52, 55-60
- Gender-inclusive housing, 19-20, 31-32, 50, 56, 75
- Restroom facilities, 19, 23, 46, 51-52, 55-56, 60, 64, 85

Adaptive Framework, 13-14
Admissions Practices (Standard 3), 17-25
- Application review process, 20-21
- Assessment and growth, 24-25
- Campus visits and tours, 19-20
- Community engagement, 24
- Electronic transactions, 17-18
- Internal communications, 22-23
- Leadership, 22
- Print communications, 18-19
- Training and professional Development, 21-22
- Work environment and culture, 23

Affinity Groups
- Employee resource groups, 46
- Student organizations, 19-20, 24, 32, 38

All-Gender Facilities
- Restrooms, 19, 23, 46, 51-52, 55-56, 60, 64, 85
- Changing rooms, 33, 46, 51, 55-56, 59
- Housing, 19-20, 31-32, 50, 56

Assessment
- Climate assessments, 37-38, 46, 52, 68, 79, 85
- Continuous improvement, 13-14, 24, 30, 67-68, 81-82
- Data collection, 38, 52, 78-83
- Longitudinal tracking, 78-83

Athletics and Recreation, 33-34, 50

B
Belonging, 14-15, 89-92
Benefits and Compensation
- Employee assistance programs, 43-44
- Family benefits, 43-44
- Gender-affirming healthcare, 44-45, 72, 74

Bias
- Incident reporting, 35, 47, 51, 69
- Mitigation strategies, 62, 84-85
- Response protocols, 34-35, 46-47, 51, 54, 68-69, 72
- Training, 19-21, 34-35, 39-40, 44-46, 53-54, 65, 83-84

C
Campus Navigation and Wayfinding, 57-58
Campus Spaces (Standard 9), 55-60
- Restroom & changing facilities, 55-56
- Residential space, 56
- Learning environments, 57
- Campus navigation & wayfinding, 57-58
- Symbolic & representational elements, 58
- Community & social spaces, 32, 58-59
- Health & wellness spaces, 59, 71-76
- Safety & security, 59-60

Career Services, 33-34
Chosen Names
- Administrative systems, 18-19, 72
- Application processes, 18-19
- Record keeping, 63

Classroom Environment, 27-30
Community Engagement, 24, 66

Confidentiality
- Healthcare services, 59, 73
- Record keeping, 73, 79-80

Continuous Improvement, 13-14, 24, 30, 67, 81-82
Counseling Services, 40-41, 59, 64, 72-73, 75
Crisis Response, 34-35, 68-69, 72
Cultural Change, 11-12
Curriculum and Pedagogy (Standard 4) 27-30
- Assessment and continuous improvement, 30
- Classroom environment, 29-30
- Curricular content, 27-28
- Faculty development, 28-29
- Inclusive pedagogy, 28-30
- Pedagogical practice, 28

D

Data Collection and Assessment (Standard 12), 77-82
- Assessment design, 79
- Continuous improvement, 81-82
- Data analysis and reporting, 79-80
- Data usage and impact, 80
- Identity data collection, 77-78
- Privacy protection, 78
- Research ethics, 81
- Transparency and communication, 80-81

Disability, 38-40, 73
Discrimination
- Non-discrimination policies, 32, 47, 49-51, 86
- Reporting mechanisms, 51

E

Electronic Systems
- Administrative records, 50-51, 63, 73
- Application portals, 17-18
- Communication platforms, 63

Emergency Procedures, 35, 57, 58-59
Employee Recruitment
- Climate and community, 46-47
- Hiring practices, 43-44
- Onboarding, 44
- Professional development, 45-46

Executive Search Firms (Standard 13), 83-87
- Firm capacity and training, 83-84
- Candidate sourcing and outreach, 84
- Search process management, 84-85
- Candidate support and advocacy, 85
- Client education and consultation, 85-86
- Accountability and continuous improvement, 86
- Post-placement support, 87

F

Facilities (Standard 9), 55-59
- All-gender restrooms, 19, 23, 46, 51, 55-56, 60, 64, 85
- Campus infrastructure, 51-52
- Residential spaces, 56

Faculty Development, 28-29
Financial Aid, 38

G

Gender Expression
- Definition, 10
- Policies supporting, 50, 57-58

Gender Identity
- Accommodations, 64
- Bias, 32, 51
- Compensation, 45
- Definition, 10
- Data analysis, 79-80
- Data collection, 52, 77-78
- Housing, 32
- Medical and Health, 72-73
- Non-discrimination, 49-50
- Privacy protection, 78
- Programming, 34
- Protections, 47
- Record systems, 20, 49-50

Gender-Inclusive Mindset, 12-13
Gender Markers
- Administrative systems, 44, 47
- Update processes, 49-50

Grievance Procedures, 51

H

Health and Wellness Services (Standard 11), 71-76
- Accessibility, 73
- Confidentiality and privacy, 73
- Gender-affirming care, 71-72
- Mental health support, 72
- Staff training, 73
- Support Networks, 75

Housing
- Assignment processes, 32, 56
- Gender-inclusive options, 31, 55-56
- Residential life policies, 32

Human Resources
- Benefits and compensation, 45
- Policy development, 51-52
- Training programs, 34, 44-46, 65-66

I
Implementation Strategies, 6-7
Inclusive Language
- Communication standards, 17-19, 62-63
- Marketing materials, 18, 33, 58, 62
- Policy documents, 28, 50, 63

Institutional Policies (Standard 8), 49-54
- Development processes, 53
- External engagement, 54
- Facilities, 51-52
- Grievance processes, 51
- Leadership, 53-54
- Non-discrimination, 49-50
- Review procedures, 53
- Records, 50-51

International Students, 39
Intersectionality (Standard 6), 37-40
- Assessment considerations, 37-38
- Healthcare and wellness, 40
- Institutional Advocacy, 41
- Programming and Community, 39
- Programming approaches, 39
- Resource allocation, 38-39
- Training and Professional Development, 39-40

J
Job Postings, 43-44, 49

L
Leadership
- Accountability, 47
- Admissions, 22
- Assessment, 53-54
- Courageous leadership, 90-91
- Development programs, 39-41, 45-46
- Executive recruitment, 83-87
- Governance structures, 53-54
- Organizational units, 62
- Student applications, 20
- Student organizations, 32
- Support and community, 46-47

Legal Considerations
- Non-discrimination policies, 32, 47, 49-50
- Title IX compliance, 51
- Executive Search, 83-84, 86

M
Mental Health Services, 40, 45, 59, 72, 74
Microaggressions, 23, 40

N
Name Changes
- Administrative processes, 47, 50-51, 67
- Admissions, 21
- Legal names, 18-19, 63, 73, 78
- Staff development, 34, 65
- System updates, 49-50

Non-Binary Identities
- Communication, 18-19
- Data collection, 77-78
- Language, 74
- Mental health support, 72

O
Offices, Centers, and Departments (Standard 10), 61-69
- Leadership and governance, 62
- Communication and language practices, 62-63
- Service delivery and programming, 63-64
- Physical environment and accessibility, 64-65
- Staff training and development, 65
- Community building and outreach, 66
- Resource allocation and support, 67
- Assessment and continuous improvement, 67-68
- Crisis response and support, 68-69

Onboarding Processes, 21, 44, 65
Orientation Programs, 19, 33-34, 44, 65,

P
Pedagogical Practices, 28, 30, 90
Performance Evaluation, 22, 45, 47, 54, 62, 65-66

Policies and Procedures, (Standard 8), 49-54
- Development, 53, 80
- Implementation, 49-54
- Review processes, 50, 53

Privacy Protection
- Culture, 23
- Data systems, 37-38, 52, 67-68, 73, 78
- Healthcare records, 72
- Healthcare, 59
- Professional development, 34
- Residence life, 31-32
- Restrooms, 55-56

Professional Development
- Faculty training, 28-29
- Staff training, 21-22

Pronouns
- Administrative systems, 17-18, 62
- Communication practices, 10, 18-23 44
- Confidentiality, 73
- Data systems, 63, 67, 84
- Leadership, 22
- Internal communications, 22-23, 72
- Pedagogical practice, 28
- Staff training, 21, 34

R
Record Keeping
- Academic records, 50-51
- Privacy protocols, 50-51, 73, 77-78
- System updates, 50-51, 63

Recruiting and Retaining (Standard 7), 43-47
- Benefits and compensation, 45-
- Employee hiring, 22, 41, 43-45, 74, 85-87
- Onboarding and integration, 44
- Policy and accountability, 47
- Recruitment and hiring, 43-44
- Support and community, 46-47
- Training, professional development and knowledge building, 45-46
- Workplace climate, 46

Research Ethics, 81
Residence Life, 31-32, 75
Restroom Facilities
- All-gender options, 19, 23, 46, 51-52, 55-56, 85
- Campus mapping, 19, 64
- Design standards, 46
- Privacy, 59-60

S
Safety and Security
- Campus navigation, 57-60
- Campus safety, 34-35
- Crisis response, 35
- Privacy, 64-65, 78

Search Committees, 44, 84-85
Signage
- Campus wayfinding, 20, 55-58, 62-64, 91
- Facility identification, 52, 55-56

Student Life (Standard 5), 31-34
- Athletics and recreation, 33
- Campus activities and events, 32-33
- Crisis response and safety, 35
- Organizations and leadership, 32
- Professional development, 34-35
- Residence life, 31-32
- Support services and programming, 33-34, 90

Student Organizations
- Collaborations, 24, 74
- Funding, 32
- Opportunities, 19-20, 24, 58-59
- Self-Assessment, 32
- Spaces, 58

Support Services
- Counseling, 40, 59, 64, 72-73
- Health services, 40, 45, 59, 71-76
- Programming and awareness, 34

Systemic Change, 9, 11-12, 37, 90-92

T
Title IX, 51
Training Programs
- Faculty development, 28-29
- Professional development, 21-22, 28-29, 34-35, 39-40, 45-46, 65-67, 73
- Staff education, 21-22, 34-35, 65, 67, 73

Transformative Change, 3, 11-12, 14, 90-92

U
Universal Design for Learning, 29-30, 90

V-W
Website Content
- Equal opportunity, 50
- Inclusive language, 6, 17-18, 58, 62

WPATH Standards of Care, 71-72
Workplace Climate, 46, 68, 79

www.ingramcontent.com/pod-product-compliance
Lightning Source LLC
Chambersburg PA
CBHW042358030426
42337CB00032B/5146